"I have a fantasy," Max murmured

Gently he played with the entwined gold chains resting on Samantha's neck. Tracing them down between her breasts, he hooked a finger over the cool metal links.

She inhaled an unsteady breath and waited for him to continue.

"The first day I met you, you were wearing this necklace." His voice dropped to a mesmerizing whisper. "It had caught around your breast—like this."

Samantha nodded, swallowing with difficulty.

"Since that day, I've had a fantasy that one day I'd make love to you. And the only thing you'd be wearing would be these chains...."

THE AUTHOR

When Marion Smith Collins was seven years old, her prizewinning school essay was published in the local paper. Since then, she admits, "The thrill of seeing my words on a printed page has never faded." After selling her first romance novel, Marion realized that her true vocation was romance writing. "Now I've found my niche, my passion," she says. "I want to do this every day for the rest of my life."

Books by Marion Smith Collins

HARLEQUIN TEMPTATION

5–BY MUTUAL CONSENT
22–BY ANY OTHER NAME
35–THIS THING CALLED LOVE

These books may be available at your local bookseller.

This Thing Called Love

MARION SMITH COLLINS

Harlequin Books

TORONTO • NEW YORK • LONDON
AMSTERDAM • PARIS • SYDNEY • HAMBURG
STOCKHOLM • ATHENS • TOKYO • MILAN

In memory of
Delores Pallet Chandler,
a beautiful and accomplished lady...
with gratitude for her confidence

Published November 1984

ISBN 0-373-25135-1

Printed in Canada

1

"NOT 'BA-BEE'!" proclaimed the shaggy-haired young man on lead guitar. "Ba-beh!"

Samantha Hyatt struck a chord on the old upright piano and wondered what the hell she was doing here. "Ba-beh," she sang in her husky contralto. "I can't help—"

"No, no, no!" The musician pulled the woven strap of the guitar over his head with barely restrained impatience, further ruffling his light hair. Laying the instrument carefully on top of a speaker, he approached the piano and perched one hip on a wooden utility stool to look down at Samantha.

His gaze was kind, but she squirmed like a student about to be reprimanded for something she couldn't help.

There was a rueful look in his eyes as he shook his head. "Not 'can't help,'" he mocked gently. "You've got to sing *country,* and that's 'cain't hep.'" He hooked the heels of his well-worn boots on the rail of the stool and leaned forward, hands clasped loosely between his knees. "Miss Hyatt, bad as I need a keyboard man, uh, person, this just ain't gonna work."

Samantha let out a long tired breath. Crossing her arms on the music shelf she rested her forehead on her arms. From both sides the dark auburn hair swung forward to hide her face, and her shoulders began to shake with helpless abandon.

The musician's boots hit the floor. "Miss Hyatt! Don't cry!" His horrified voice came from only a step away. "We'll try again, maybe. But please, don't cry!"

Samantha lifted her head to grin at him. Her amber eyes were dry. "Oh, Johnny," she said with a laugh. "I'm not crying, just disgusted with myself. You're right. This won't work."

Johnny gave her a rather sheepish smile. "You're one helluva piano player, Miss Hyatt, but a lousy country singer."

"I know," she responded. "But I've enjoyed trying...I think." She looked around at the other members of the group. The handsome drummer met her smile with one of real regret. He had been coming on to her from the moment the audition began, all of fifteen minutes ago. "Thanks, boys," she said to them.

"Uh, Miss Hyatt, if you still need a job...." His eyes skidded bashfully over her expensive outfit—the raw silk slacks, rust-colored sweater of loosely woven cotton, gold chains plaited around her neck and the gold bangle bracelet—before returning to meet her stare.

She had known from the moment she parked her car outside the rather rustic building that her clothes were inappropriate for this audition, but by then it had been too late to go home and change. It was clear, however, that she hadn't lost the chance for the job because of what she wore. Johnny was flatteringly appreciative of her talent. She focused her attention again on the question he'd asked.

Need a job? Maybe not to eat, at least not for the

immediate present. But as a reason, a purpose for living, she needed one quite desperately. "Yes, I do need a job, Johnny," she told him sincerely. "Do you know of anything else?"

Johnny propped an elbow on top of the old upright and linked his long fingers together. "I heard they were looking for a piano player over at Sea Tangle, that new resort just outside of town. It's a little more high-class than this." He waved an arm to indicate the simple café and bar. "In fact, I don't know what the Red-neck Riviera is coming to with all these fancy new places springing up. It's beginning to look more like Palm Beach."

Samantha laughed with him. She had only moved to the small town of Destin, on the Gulf Coast of Florida, one month ago, but she was already familiar with the term *Red-neck Riviera,* used affectionately by the native-born residents. She had often suspected that they called it that to discourage the developers from turning their sleepy little Eden into a commercial nightmare.

Then her laughter faded and she suddenly became sober. "To play solo? I'm not sure I could do it alone, Johnny. I told you, it's been a long time since I performed at all."

She was beginning to wonder if the whole thing hadn't been a mistake, giving up a well-established career to return to her first love, music. "And please call me Samantha. Or Sam," she added automatically for the umpteenth time that morning.

"But you haven't lost your touch," Johnny went on enthusiastically, ignoring her request. "You're really great. It's just that you're not country." He grinned, showing the whitest teeth she'd ever seen, and spread his hands palms up with a resigned shrug. "I...oh hell, we all wish you were. Believe me, you'd give us good old boys some style; but the job at Sea Tangle sounds more like your thing."

"Well, I suppose I could try." *Playing piano... alone...in a bar,* she thought doubtfully. At least here a semblance of security existed in the presence of the others; at least there was a pretense of a dining room, although the sign outside put less emphasis on "Oyster" than on "Bar." Flashing red-and-yellow lights on a portable marquee announced that a dozen on the half shell and all the beer one could drink was only five dollars on Saturday night. "I'm beginning to think I should have stayed in Illinois," she told Johnny with a self-deprecating smile.

"Why did you come south?" he asked with unabashed curiosity. Once more he relaxed his lanky frame against the edge of the wooden stool.

Samantha smiled to herself. In their very brief acquaintance she had discovered that he never stood alone if he could lean or prop. "I got tired of shoveling snow," she told him. No need to go into the deeper reasons. She stood up and reached for her purse on top of the piano. As she pulled it toward her it dislodged a billow of dust, prompting three violent sneezes in rapid succession.

Johnny laughed. "You see, you're probably allergic to the Oyster Bar's housekeeping, too."

Samantha sniffed inelegantly and smiled through watery eyes. "I'll drive out to Sea Tangle right now to see if they've dusted their piano. Thanks for the audition, Johnny, and for the tip."

"Good luck, Miss Hyatt. If you get the job, me and the boys'll come hear you play one night."

"Sam," she corrected him firmly. "And I'll be back to hear Johnny and the Rural Route, too. Bye." She smiled at herself for the southern farewell and waved as she threaded her way through the tables to the front door.

She supposed she could always teach.

"THIS IS OUR NEW LOUNGE, Miss Hyatt." The well-groomed man in the three-piece suit had introduced himself as Monty Patton. He unhooked a gold velvet rope, let Samantha through and refastened it. "As you can see, we're not quite through with the decorating, but we'll be ready to open in a few days."

He led the way down two steps from the lobby to a now-deserted area dominated by a magnificent ten-foot piano bar of gleaming dark mahogany. It was positioned so that the pianist's back would be to a wall of glass overlooking the blue waters of the Gulf. Dark green leather stools were grouped around the long curve of the bar itself.

The rest of the room was haphazardly arranged with puffy sofas and comfortable chairs upholstered in subtle shades of peach and green, still swathed in their clear plastic covers for protection. Natural-cane tables with glass tops were bunched in one corner. Ceiling fans had been installed. She could imagine them moving in lazy circles, barely stirring the fronds of feather palms. The entire setting would be a welcome oasis for hotel guests after a day spent under the hot Florida sun.

Samantha turned slowly. "It's really lovely," she told the man.

He beamed proudly. "Thank you."

On another wall was a business bar of the same

gleaming mahogany as the piano. Soft lighting illuminated the mirrored shelves, which held an assortment of shining glassware. Except for the scattered furniture and bare concrete floors, everything seemed to be in readiness.

The lounge area was separated from the main lobby not by walls, but by lacy wrought iron, giving it the effect of being a part of, but separate from, the bustling heart of the hotel.

Samantha felt her excitement growing. Johnny was right. She would love to work here. From the moment she'd cleared the well-guarded gates, she had begun to appreciate the understated elegance of Sea Tangle. The drive curved and turned under large, moss-hung oak trees and through meticulously maintained gardens to emerge into the courtyard of the modern eight-story hotel.

"The boss wants someone who can play quiet background music." Monty Patton's voice recalled Samantha from her wandering speculations. "You know—show tunes, old favorites. He says that for what that piano cost him, he doesn't want anyone banging out rock and roll on it. Do you sing?"

Samantha smiled and dropped her purse onto a chair. She was magnetically drawn to the beautiful instrument. "Yes, but I play better," she said. She ran her fingers lightly over the keys. *Perfectly in tune—beautiful tone,* she thought, but she dared not let herself hope until she'd met the boss.

"Why don't you try out the piano? I'll go look for Mr. Townsend."

"Fine." Samantha tried not to let all of her enthusiasm show. She sat down at the instrument, made a slight adjustment to the seat and flexed her fingers.

Her touch was light, her technique perfect. The movement of her fingers merged effortlessly with the expertise in her head to bring forth a medley of songs from a Broadway show of a decade ago.

It was Samantha's habit to play the piano each day, if only for a few minutes. In the six years since she'd last studied she'd never let herself get rusty. It had always been a comfort to have her music to fall back on. Even during the difficult days when she had agonized over the decision to leave Illinois and her job, the piano had been her release, her tranquilizer.

Her eyes drifted shut as she plucked the notes of "Summertime" from her memory. She played it more slowly than some, her rendition haunting and sentimental. The piano was in perfect tune and, as she played, the music seemed to stretch, to flow into every corner of the room with the undulating rhythm that George Gershwin had written into it years ago.

The dimple in her cheek became a shadowed hollow as she switched to her own sensual rendition of "As Time goes By." Her friends had always said it should be her theme song, but she'd never been tempted to succumb to the obvious.

SAMANTHA WASN'T AWARE of the picture she presented to the man who had entered the room and stood quietly watching from behind the bar. Her hair was loose almost to her waist, and had turned to live flame by the setting sun behind her. Seen in profile, her features were delicate and heart-catchingly beautiful, he thought, surprised at the sudden jump his pulse took.

He moved farther to the right to get a full-faced view. Sliding one hand into the pocket of his jeans he rested his other forearm on the bar, listening and looking.

Long lashes settled like velvet on her cheeks. Her short straight nose led his eyes to a rather full upper lip, lightly glossed. The lower lip, parted from its mate enough to show a glimpse of even white teeth, was a perfect arc. In all his life he had never seen a mouth just like that—sexy as hell and just begging to be kissed.

He made a conscious effort to drop his gaze from those amazing lips to her firm chin. In contrast to a rather stubborn inclination there, the concave curve to her throat was curiously vulnerable. His eyes traveled further down to the deep shadow at the V neck of her sweater.

He felt an unexpected stirring in his loins when his visual exploration reached her breasts. Several long chains were twisted together around her neck to form a gold rope. With her movements the gold had shifted to one side and was caught under one upthrust mound. He watched in fascination, waiting for a shift of her body to free it, until finally, frowning at where his thoughts were taking him, he straightened.

Abstractedly, he put out his hand for the clean white cloth folded on the bar in front of him. He began to wipe. Two steps to the left brought him again to a view of her profile.

Her waist was tiny like the rest of her. Her sweetly rounded derriere shifted slightly each time she stretched her toes to a pedal or reached for a chord on the keyboard.

He couldn't judge her height from the seated position because her legs seemed long in proportion to her diminutive size. Her hands were hidden by the edge of the piano, but he could picture them—graceful, with tapered fingers as befitted this delightful fairylike creature.

The hand on the cloth retreated to stroke his full mustache as he tried to rationalize his reaction to the lovely woman. He was certainly no stranger to beautiful women. They abounded here on the northern coast of the gulf. But there was something different about this one, something almost ethereal.

As the last notes of the song faded away, she opened her eyes and slowly turned her head to meet his gaze.

Without any warning he felt his breath, caught by an unseen hand within his chest, fighting to be free. He was drawn by invisible strings into the aura that radiated from the woman's amber eyes. There was no surprise in her expression. It was as though she knew he'd been watching her.

Automatically one hand reached for the cloth again and the other came out of the pocket of his jeans to clench in a fist on the edge of the bar. How odd. He hadn't had this kind of instant reaction to a woman in years, this "across a crowded room" feeling. In fact, he couldn't remember ever having it to this degree. His excitement was tempered with the remarkable sensation that he needed the expanse of wood between them as a shield.

SAMANTHA FELT the presence of the man a split second before she opened her eyes. She almost gasped aloud at the latent virility that seemed to reach out for her.

The blood in her veins grew thick, slowing her heartbeat to a leaden drumming resonant in her ears.

Her fingers dropped from the keys to rest in her lap, and she linked them loosely together while she continued to tolerate his stare. Tolerate? Whom was she trying to fool? She was reveling in it. She let her breath out in a soft stream, hoping he wouldn't notice the sigh.

The man was gorgeous, but if there was one thing she didn't need in her life at this particular time, it was a gorgeous man. Especially one who caught her gaze in the depths of the clearest bluest eyes she'd ever seen—and refused to let go.

All at once he smiled, a warm tender smile, as though he knew her thoughts, and she groaned silently at the unexpected flutter she felt deep within her body. *Not now, for heaven's sake!*

The woman who stood so abruptly was not Samantha Hyatt: piano player in search of a job. She was Dr. Samantha Hyatt: psychologist, retired or on sabbatical or...something. Dr. Hyatt wasn't about to be attracted to a handsome face. That fact should be made absolutely clear right now.

She smoothed palms that were none too dry down the side seams of her slacks and sauntered casually over to the bar. "Hello," she said too curtly. "I presume you are the bartender?" She really hadn't meant for the question to come out as a challenge, but it sounded like one, she realized belatedly.

At her brusque tone the blue eyes narrowed. She watched a muscle jump in his jaw but the man didn't speak. He merely gave a careless nod and picked up the towel.

She was dismayed to discover that at close range he was even better looking, despite the fact that he had a mustache. She'd never like mustaches or men who wore them. In her opinion mustaches were childish efforts by rather ordinary men to prove their machismo. "See," they seemed to be saying, "I can grow hair on my face and you can't." However, this particular visage didn't owe its masculinity to any device.

The blaze of sunset from the window to his left kissed the rugged planes of his face, shadowed the shallow cleft in his strong chin and deepened the golden highlights in his toast-colored hair. His lashes were thick and surprisingly dark. The white dress shirt he wore was open at the throat, giving her a glimpse of tanned skin sprinkled generously with curly hair.

He had the build of a well-conditioned athlete, but the first intimation she had of his size was when she realized that her eyes were on a level with the second button of his shirt. She raised them to the broad expanse of his shoulders, and all at once was glad for the width of the bar between them.

Placing both hands on a stool behind her she lifted herself to perch on the edge. It wasn't that she felt threatened by his size, she told herself, but the extra inches added to her self-confidence. "I'm Samantha Hyatt," she told him.

He gave the spotless surface a slow circular swipe, following the trail of the cloth with his eyes.

"I'm applying for the pianist's job," she told him, and still got no reaction. "We might be working together." Silence.

What was the matter with the man? Thirty seconds ago he had seemed...well, interested at least, and now he was totally ignoring her. The idea that he could become so suddenly dismissive peeved her for some reason, but she didn't stop to analyze why. Instead she propped her chin on the heel of her hand and rested her elbow on the bar. She looked up at him through her thick lashes, resisting the urge to bat them and see what would happen. "The stereotyped bartender is supposed to be a born psychologist," she informed him.

At that he finally looked at her. One corner of his mouth quivered with the suggestion of laughter struggling to be free, and a dark brow lifted in silent question. She interpreted the expression as a smirk, and it increased her annoyance. She went on in a much cooler voice. "Of course, no one really believes that, except maybe the bartenders themselves." He still didn't say a word.

Her eyes were drawn to the slow hypnotic movement of his hand and the towel. His wrist was strong looking. The forearm was dense with sinew and the hair growing there lay flat below the rolled-back cuffs as though determined to be civilized. Idly she wondered if it was as soft as it looked; she recalled herself with horror. The hand holding up her chin dropped and she crossed her arms on the counter.

There was something almost mesmerizing about the slow easy movement of the towel, she thought crossly, as he continued to wipe. "You're going to wear a hole in the wood," she snapped. "It looks clean enough to me."

She forced her eyes to meet his but the expression there was unreadable. If he was offended by her remarks he gave no sign. Indeed he seemed almost indifferent. What was the man doing to her? And why was she reacting this way?

Samantha caught her breath. Suddenly she knew what he was *trying* to do and she wanted to laugh out loud. He was playing psychologist! The first rule of therapy: let the subject open up to you. Be receptive. He was actually trying to teach her a lesson! How taken aback he would be if he knew he was dealing with a professional.

She lifted a hand to hide her grin behind her fingers. She knew the rules all right but they didn't apply to her, she thought dismissively. A professional rose above the rules.

Well, two could play at this game. She decided to goad him further. "I suppose people pour out all their fantasies to you. You probably hear some wild stories."

That earned her a grin, which she ignored and went on recklessly. "That's very dangerous, you know. If someone really needed professional help you could give them a false sense of security." Again her gaze was drawn to the hand holding the towel and again it was an effort to draw her eyes away. His fingers were long and well-shaped, the nails clipped neatly, and he handled the towel with a sure touch. He would probably handle a woman the same way, smoothly and with finesse. She could almost feel....

This had gone on long enough! Samantha slid off the stool. "Actually the bartenders I've known haven't been very intelligent." As a parting shot it couldn't be bettered, she thought smugly as she started to walk away, but then she heard the deep masculine chuckle from behind her.

"And how many bartenders have you been intimately acquainted with, Miss Samantha Hyatt?"

At the first sound of that warm and husky southern drawl Samantha spun around and her heart dropped to her toes. With a blinding flash of insight she realized she had been neatly maneuvered.

He hadn't even made a fool of her; she'd done that very well without help. He had simply let her rattle on to prove his point. She had been the one who had thought she was above breaking the rules of therapy. The deplorable man had let her open her mouth and then put her foot in it!

Embarrassment warred with anger at herself and won easily to color her face. There was absolutely no graceful way out of this situation. "I...uh...." What could she say? She dropped her eyes from his lips, which were curved with amusement, to study the toe of her shoe. "None," she finally admitted in a soft voice.

He moved so quietly that she had no hint of his approach until the brown-leather deck shoes appeared in her line of vision. Reluctantly and slowly she let her eyes travel up his muscular legs encased in the tight jeans, over his lean hips and flat stomach until they reached his belt buckle. The journey did nothing to cool the heat in her cheeks.

The large hand she had watched in such fascination was extended. "I'm Max Stanwood."

She hesitated only for a second before placing her own in it. Her fingers were immediately swallowed up.

"Now you do," he said mysteriously.

She lifted her puzzled gaze to his. "Now I do what?" she asked vaguely. He *was* big—at least a foot taller than her diminutive five foot one. But, to her surprise, she didn't feel threatened at all. Rather she felt an odd sort of protective warmth radiating from his body.

"Now you know a bartender," he explained simply. But with a deliberately seductive smile he added, "Maybe you don't know him intimately... yet... but you know one."

Samantha's embarrassment at being caught showing off evaporated at the typically macho statement. She pulled her hand free and straightened to her full height. "*Yet,* Mr. Stanwood? You flatter yourself." She drew the words out in an ominous tone and would have continued to take a piece off his arrogant hide, but fortunately for the man in front of her, they were interrupted. At least she told herself that the good fortune was on his side. If she was being absolutely honest, however, she would have to admit to a feeling of relief. Max Stanwood was a worthy opponent.

Monty Patton bustled down the two steps followed by a balding man in his sixties who was introduced as Mr. Townsend.

Samantha presented the bartender her back as she shook hands with the owner of the hotel. Only after their greetings were exchanged did she risk a glance over her shoulder to find that Mr. Stanwood had done a quick disappearing act. He probably didn't want the boss to catch him loitering, she thought with satisfaction.

The audition would have been over almost as soon as she sat down at the keyboard, but Mr. Townsend was enthralled with her playing and didn't want her to stop. He even liked her imperfect voice, and she was thoroughly charmed by his courtly manner.

"In my day we called that a 'whiskey voice,' Miss Hyatt," he told her when she disparaged her singing. "I knew a lot of vocalists who would have envied you."

"Please call me Samantha, Mr. Townsend. Or Sam, if you prefer. Is there anything else you'd like me to play?"

Samantha was more than happy to render each of his requests, especially on such a beautiful instrument. When she told him so he was delighted. "The piano was my wife's idea, really," he admitted. "She will be thrilled when she hears you play, Samantha. Can you start on Friday?" He turned to his manager who hovered on the periphery of their conversation. "Will the room be ready by Friday, Monty?"

"Yes, sir," Monty assured his boss with the deference of a buck private to a five-star general. "The rush matting for the floor will be installed tomorrow."

"Good." He turned back to Samantha and was suddenly all business. "Now, Samantha, we will want you to play from four-thirty until nine—everyone will have moved into the dining room by then, or if they haven't they should have. We have a club downstairs for entertainment and dancing after the dinner hour." He smiled and Samantha liked him even better for the comment. Apparently he didn't expect her to play for customers who would rather drink than eat. "Six nights a week, Sundays off. You'll have one Saturday free each month." He named a salary figure that startled her.

"That sounds very generous, Mr. Townsend. Thank you."

Her surprise must have been evident for he laughed. "I pay all my employees well, Samantha. I find that it makes for better relations."

"I'm sure it does," she agreed. The psychologist in Samantha recognized that Mr. Townsend was buying loyalty, but she would be willing to wager that it was effective. He probably had very little employee turnover. Again she thanked her lucky stars that she had come to Sea Tangle.

They shook hands on the verbal arrangement and she promised to appear two days from now at twenty minutes after four.

When she left the hotel her step was light and joyous. This job was exactly what she'd been hoping to find. How lucky for her that Johnny had known about it. She gave the doorman a cheerful salute and hurried to her car.

She couldn't help the smile of satisfaction the sight of the Mercedes gave her. It had been the first step in her change to a new life-style.

"Totally impractical and ridiculously extravagant," Gregory had proclaimed. At the thought of Gregory her brow furrowed. She climbed into the car and started the engine. Gregory was part of yesterday. He had never belonged in her life and why she hadn't seen that sooner she would never know. As she accelerated out of the parking lot her memory provided a glimpse of a tall figure in jeans and a white shirt. She wondered what Gregory would think of Max Stanwood.

During the conversation with Mr. Townsend she had completely dismissed the rude bartender from her mind... well, almost completely. Once or twice her eyes had inadvertently strayed to the door behind the bar but he had not reappeared. She tried to tell herself that she was relieved, but a smidgen of truthfulness compelled her to admit disappointment.

That sharp knowing response she'd felt when their eyes met for the first time worried her a bit and brought on a strange, almost claustrophobic breathlessness. But Samantha was sure she could avoid anything remotely resembling Stage One of a romantic entanglement if she put her mind to it.

Her life was just now taking on the shape she'd planned two months ago when she'd decided to restructure it. She wasn't about to get involved with a man until she was completely settled and comfortable in her new surroundings. Maybe not even then, she amended. Men were trouble.

2

TWO DAYS LATER Samantha was still repeating those words to herself as she walked into the lounge at Sea Tangle. She looked around at the transformed room. It was just as she had been picturing it in her mind since Wednesday, down to the man behind the bar.

Max Stanwood was smiling at something a hefty man on the barstool in front of him had said. The sight of him, that relaxed easy manner of a man totally comfortable in his surroundings, tripped her heartbeat. She suspected that Max wouldn't bother with unnecessary gestures or movements.

When he spied her the smile widened to a grin and he gave the "thumbs up" sign. Apparently he had decided to forget the antagonism between them.

Samantha answered with a nervous smile that wasn't wholly due to her fear of the coming performance. The silly man had haunted her thoughts and even shown up once in her dreams, darn him!

Lifting her chin resolutely, she walked on stiff legs toward the piano, smiling woodenly at the sprinkling of customers already gathered in the room. She slid her small black purse under the edge of the bench and sat down. *Here goes nothing,* she thought, her whole body tense with apprehension.

All afternoon she had been trying to remember the notes of songs she'd played for years, but the anticipation of playing and singing in front of people again, not to mention the presence of the hulk who loomed behind the bar, had numbed her brain to an utter void.

She rubbed her palms together and licked lips that were arid and parched.

"How about something to drink before you begin?"

The deep voice startled her into a sharp reply. "I don't think so." Then in a milder tone, "Thanks, anyway." She risked a glance at him.

Today his shirt was blue and it deepened the color of his eyes to a startling indigo. He wore a white bar apron tied casually around his narrow waist. What should have been a feminine accoutrement only served to emphasize the dynamic virility that Samantha had hoped to discover was an illusion. She couldn't have been more wrong, she realized, finding her eyes drawn to the wrinkled strings knotted over his flat stomach.

He stood over her, his hands resting loosely at his hips, his smile slightly crooked as he waited calmly. "Water? Coke?" he prompted.

A curvaceous young girl in a short skirt and long black stockings walked by carrying a tray of empty glasses. She gave Samantha a curious look and said, "Max. Refills."

"In a minute. Come here, Barbara."

The girl stopped dead in her tracks and backed up with a peculiar little shuffling step. "Yes, Master."

Max frowned at her flippancy. "Samantha, this is Barbara Howard. Barbara, Samantha Hyatt, the new pianist. The other girl over there is the second bartender, Barbara's sister, Jenny."

Samantha hadn't noticed anyone else, but as her gaze followed the direction of his arm she saw that they were being watched.

Barbara's sister appeared to be a few years older. They were both blondes, but where Barbara's hair was full and blowsy, Jenny's was cut short, a neat cap on her head. Samantha's tentative smile was returned with one of real warmth.

"Pleased to meet you," said the younger girl, recalling Samantha's attention. She didn't sound pleased at all.

"I'm happy to meet you, too." Samantha responded mechanically. She wasn't sure she was pleased, either. There seemed to be a strain of possessiveness in the girl's attitude toward Max. She frowned. What difference could that possibly make to her?

"Max. Refills," Barbara reminded sharply and walked away.

"I'll be right there," Max told her and turned back to Samantha. "Come on. You've got to do something to relax. You're as taut as a bowstring." His voice had lowered to a level that wouldn't be overheard and she matched hers to it.

"Does it show that badly?" She looked up into the depths of his eyes, seeking reassurance and not even aware of how incongruous it was for her to seek it from him.

The corners of his mouth tugged into a smile. "No," he consoled gently. "Not to someone who hadn't witnessed your affinity for this instrument. But today you approached it as though it was the guillotine."

Samantha chuckled and looked down at the keys.

"Maybe I feel that way, Max." She missed his indrawn breath. "I haven't played before an audience in six years." She spread her hands and looked up again. "Is it any wonder I'm nervous?"

He didn't ask why she hadn't played. Instead his smile widened to that perceptive grin. "If you play one-tenth as good as you look, Sam, we won't have room for all the people who will flock in here to see you once word gets around the hotel."

"Thank you, sir." She was ridiculously pleased and curiously reassured by the compliment. She had taken great pains with her appearance this afternoon. Her dark auburn hair was clean and shining and had been brushed until it framed her face and spilled down her back like a cloud. Mr. Townsend hadn't specified what she was to wear and so she tried to look natural and comfortable but chic. Her dress was a black-and-white geometric print of cotton piqué. Strapless, it clung to the upper half of her body like another skin. A wide belt of black grosgrain defined her waist and the skirt belled to her knees. She wore sandals with thin black straps and high heels.

Max hadn't missed a single detail during his slow inventory. She sat very still and listened to her heart drum in her ears. When he spoke again he sounded slightly hoarse. "You're sure that dress will stay up?"

"Positive," she promised. Her own voice was none too steady. She could almost feel the touch of his gaze and it left her skin warm and sensitive.

"Okay. I'll take your word for it, but I wasn't hired for this job to be a bouncer, too." He took a long breath and tore his eyes away from the curve of her bare shoulders. "Now, about that drink...?"

"Water is fine," she told him quietly.

When he returned with a small tray it held not only a tall glass of water garnished with a thin wedge of lime, but an empty brandy snifter which he set on the corner of the piano.

"What's that for?" she asked as she watched him dig into the pocket of his jeans.

"For your tips." He dropped a bill into the snifter. "I'm seeding the pot."

"Tips!" she hissed. "But I don't...I've never—"

"Sh-sh," he interrupted with a frown. "All piano bars have them."

"Take it away," she ordered. "I'm being well paid. I don't have to be tipped." The idea made her uncomfortable.

A gleam of suspicion lit his eyes for a moment and was gone. "Nope," he said cheerfully. "Give it to your favorite charity if you like, but it stays." He leaned an elbow on the edge of the piano and lowered his voice to a sensual purr. "And now for my request. Play something slow and sexy, Sam, and let me imagine what it will be like to taste that beautiful mouth."

Samantha watched him with wide eyes and a slack jaw as he straightened and sauntered back to the bar. He did have an attractive.... Samantha jerked her attention from the insufferable man's behind and lifted her hands to the keyboard. With too much vigor she started in on a bright rendition of "Cabaret."

By the time the last notes of the song were played her nervousness had disappeared. She pulled the arm of the microphone toward her mouth. "Good evening, ladies and gentlemen, I'm Samantha Hyatt...."

People drifted in and out for the next forty minutes, some walking gingerly from the effects of too much sun, some with deep golden tans, all beautifully dressed and flatteringly approving of the new pianist. A few of the male members of her audience chose the stools in the curve of the piano and she kept up a light patter with them between songs. She was always aware of the attentive vigilance of the man behind the bar. For some reason it gave her a sense of security, which effectively wiped out any lingering self-consciousness. She laughed and talked easily with the customers.

Samantha was surprised when she received the sign from Max that it was time for a break. The forty minutes of her first set had flown by. She announced that she would return in ten minutes and reached down for her purse. When she stood she found herself face-to-face with one of the customers, an older man, who was nevertheless quite attractive.

"May I buy you a drink, Miss Hyatt?" he asked.

She hesitated. She had noticed earlier that he seemed to be alone. "Well, I...."

"Miss Hyatt has a telephone call," said Max from behind the man. "I'm sure you'll excuse her." He took her arm in a firm grip and drew her forward.

Samantha tugged slightly to free herself, but after one glance at his determined jaw, abandoned her efforts. She looked back at the customer with an apologetic smile.

Max escorted her through the crowd, which had grown considerably since she had begun playing, and around behind the bar. A large hand pushed open the swinging door to the room in back. To her surprise she found herself in a comfortably furnished office.

But the decor of the room was the last thing on her mind at this point. She jerked her arm free and glared up at him. "I don't have a phone call. What's this all about?" she demanded.

Max leaned against the desk, crossing his feet at the ankles and his brawny arms across his chest. "How do you know?" he questioned smoothly.

"What?" She held her small purse in front of her like an ineffective shield.

"How do you know you don't have a call?" he repeated.

"Well, because no one—" She broke off.

"Knows where you are," he finished for her. His face hardened to a grim expression. "What are you running away from, Sam? I've been watching you. A beautiful woman like you doesn't just show up out of the blue."

"Playing psychologist again, Mr. Stanwood?" she asked sarcastically.

"I just want to know why an intelligent woman of your age would chuck everything to apply for a job that doesn't require much of her."

Before she could tell him that it was none of his business, Barbara stuck her head through the door. "Max, I have an order." She looked put out at finding the two of them together.

"Jenny can handle it. I'll be there in a minute," he snapped impatiently.

"Well, excu-use me!" said Barbara, shaking the fingers of one hand as though to dislodge something sticky. "*I'm* just doing my job." She flounced out leaving the door swinging behind her.

Max unfolded his arms to plant his hands on his hips. "Now look here, Samantha—"

"No. You look here, Mr. Stanwood. Why I'm here is none of your concern." Samantha tossed the purse onto the desk behind him and planted her fists on her hips, too. Masculine overbearance was something she could deal with quite effectively. Since meeting this man she had been off-balance, but no more, she vowed. She fixed him with her best icy frown. "You manhandle me in front of all those people, drag me back here on a flimsy pretext that there's a phone call for me. What are you trying to do?"

"Right now I'm trying to be patient with you," he grated. "It's obvious that you've never played a bar before...."

"Why is it so obvious?" she snapped.

"Because you're too damned naive!"

His voice was rising and she felt her anger readily rising to meet it. "I'm not naive! I'm twenty-nine years old. There hasn't been a naive bone in my body for years."

"About playing in a bar you are! You didn't even know what the brandy glass was for." He leaned forward until their noses were almost touching. "You've never worked for tips. The idea makes you uncomfortable. In fact, you don't know a thing about tipping. And you don't know that when you accept an invitation to drink with a customer he very well may consider you his for the rest of the evening!"

She raised her chin imperiously. "In a place like Sea Tangle? I doubt that!"

"In any place, you little fool! Look at you." He erupted then, lifting the air with his big hand, palm up. His eyes raked over her form and he was almost shouting. The outburst seemed so uncharacteristic that she stared. "You're so damned tiny I could break you with two fingers! And you're so god-damned beautiful—" He broke off. The static electricity between them crackled, filling the air. Neither could deny its charge and neither could look away.

Samantha held her breath, the golden velvet eyes huge in her face. Silence fell on the room like a heavy blanket, even muffling the sound of his harsh breathing.

Haltingly the hand that had been extended reached for her arm. Touched her briefly. Withdrew. And then returned to curve decisively around her elbow. His breathing slowed but became deeper and heavier. His voice altered. What had been a shout was now a husky rasp as he drew her gradually nearer. "So *very* beautiful."

It was the warmth of his fingers on the inside of her arm that paralyzed her. It was the fire burning in his eyes that consumed any thoughts of resistance as he matched the length of her body very carefully against his. But what was it that made her tilt her head back? Made her part her lips to catch his breath in her mouth just before he covered her lips with his? She didn't know, for she had never been affected this way before—dazed, disoriented, hungry with a singular appetite for this one man. Only he—since their eyes had first met.

Why had she thought she didn't like mustaches when the brush of his mustache across her skin was the most sensual experience she'd ever known?

His mouth was mobile, tasting her own, lightly at first, then shifting to find another angle like a starving man at a buffet table, wanting to try everything but also wanting to have his fill of what he liked most. "Sam, Sam." Her name was a litany, repeated over and over in the softest of whispers.

Suddenly his fingers tore into her hair, holding her head immobile as he feasted. His tongue plunged inside her mouth, exploring her teeth, sweeping beyond into the warm moistness, satisfied to have found the angle of deepest penetration.

Samantha's last thought before she succumbed completely to erotic sensation was that she was opening up a part of herself that had never been exposed before. And then she slid her arms around his waist and curved into him, no longer able to stand on her own under the force of the most overwhelming kiss she'd ever experienced. Her tongue joined his, as eager to taste, to explore, as he was.

Never releasing her mouth, Max stumbled back a step to come to rest against the edge of the desk. Then, wrapping her in his arms, he pulled her between his legs, toward his hard arousal.

Her breasts were crushed into his broad chest but they strained beneath the fabric for even closer contact. He sensed her need and one large hand came up to swallow her fullness in a gentle grasp. When his palm began to move over her, she felt her nipple thrust in sweet demand against its lace prison. He felt it, too, and caught the bud between his thumb and forefinger to tug lightly.

A soundless whimper broke from her throat to be captured in his mouth and she shifted, the need deep inside her seeking fulfillment.

With a hungry groan, Max wrenched his lips from hers. His hand left her breast to cradle her head under his chin, while he fought to calm the breath that stirred the hair at her temple.

Still in a daze, Samantha explored the muscles of his back with restless hands and moved her hips again, repeating her silent demand.

The arm at her back contracted. "God, darlin'! Don't do that. It feels.... Later, sweetheart. I promise you...."

Later? What was he talking about? Was he going to deny this...?

All at once lids that had been too heavy ever to lift again, popped up. The room slipped, righted itself. My God! What was she doing? Was she crazy? She winced at the phrasing. Her fingers slowly, almost painfully, released their grip on his shirt and came around to wedge between their bodies.

He didn't try to hold her except for a steadying hand at her waist as she stepped back, but frantically she slapped that away. "What do you think you're doing?" she charged, shaken to the depths by the unfamiliar emotion born of his kiss. Never. Never before had she lost control like that. Their eyes were locked and she watched the confusion in his gradually clear, to be replaced by caution.

He slid his hands into the pockets of his jeans, tightening them further, which didn't help her composure. "The question is, darlin', what were *you* doing?" he drawled huskily.

Samantha's shoulders suddenly felt the weight of guilt and mortification. She couldn't defend her actions. He was right. She had responded without reservation, wanting him at least as much as he had wanted her, or more. When she thought of the way she'd wiggled.... Dear God, had she actually done that?

She took a long calming breath, smoothed her hair back with both hands and tried for a semblance of dignity. When she spoke, her voice betrayed her befuddled senses. "Yes. Well, ah, I've never kissed a man with a mustache before. It was, ah, was...."

Max's laugh boomed out and rolled over her, adding to her embarrassment. Her fingers curled in to her palms to make fists. For an excuse, she realized it was rather weak, but it wasn't hilarious. She took a deep breath. "What's so damned funny?" she demanded, as angry with him now as she was with herself.

"You!" he whooped. "Trying to excuse...." He went off into fresh laughter. His hand came down on her shoulder, giving it an affectionate squeeze. "Darlin', there's nothing wrong...." He gasped, trying to compose himself.

She shrugged violently, dislodging his hand, and stepped back. "I suppose I should have expected mockery from a *bartender.*"

His laughter slackened, stopped. The silence that stretched between them was once again charged, but not with the electricity of desire. His eyes searched her features as though hoping to misread what he saw there.

Why did she feel like crying? She lifted her chin instead and glared at him.

His eyelids closed for a minute, then opened. The blue was now a piercing laserlike color. He was sober when he asked, "Is that what's bothering you? That you kissed a bartender?"

Samantha shrank from the derision in his eyes. No! She couldn't let him think...but wasn't that what she'd felt earlier? Her hesitation was all he needed to reinforce the hard freeze in his eyes.

A muscle in his jaw twitched. It was the only physical evidence of his anger, but she could feel the tension radiating from the large body. "For a few minutes out there, when you first came in, I thought I saw a soft, feminine, almost-vulnerable woman." His voice was dangerously low and controlled, and it sent shivers of apprehension down her back. "And when I held you in my arms just now I was sure of it. But that was all a delusion, wasn't it, Sam? You really are the cold snobbish bitch I met the first day."

His scathing denouncement ripped into Samantha like a knife slashing through tender skin. Without another word he brushed past her and out the door, leaving her stunned and hurt, deeply hurt, both by his words and by the fact that there was more than an element of truth in them.

She wasn't snobbish, was she? But she had acted like a snob. Uncertain, she looked around for a chair before her knees gave way completely. Perched on the cushion, she ran back over their conversation in her mind and she had to admit that she had sounded exactly like what he accused her of being.

The man unsettled her, made her say things she didn't mean, both today and when they'd talked on Wednesday. Or rather when she'd talked and he'd listened on Wednesday, she thought in chagrin. She remembered how neatly he'd maneuvered her then.

There was something strange about Max Stanwood, something that didn't ring true. She couldn't put her finger on what it was, but there was no trace of logic to her thoughts at the moment. All she could remember was that devastating kiss and the knowledge that she had disappointed him, and a strange sad regret for both.

Absently she glanced down at her watch and stood quickly in dismay. She was five minutes late!

When Samantha appeared two minutes later in the doorway behind the bar, her lips were freshly glossed and her hair had been brushed. If the sight of her nose in the air reinforced Max's opinion that she was a snob, that was too bad. She needed all the resolve she could collect to get through this next set. The whole scene in the office had left her emotions fluctuating erratically.

She took a step and her way was blocked by Max's big body. "Let me pass, please," she told a button on his shirt, not willing to risk looking directly at him. He would still be furious, and rightly so.

"Don't forget what I said about the customers," he ordered harshly.

That statement brought her eyes up. "I can take care of myself," she answered. "I don't need a guardian."

She could tell from his expression that he hadn't forgiven her, but there was a certain reluctant concern there. She started to say something more—not sure what the words would have been—when he turned his back on her.

"Forgive me. I keep forgetting how self-sufficient you are." His voice was so cold that she almost shivered in response.

This time she played for a full hour, ignoring Max's signal. At least sitting at the piano she didn't have to think, except about the growing number of tips in the brandy snifter. Max had been right. They disturbed her.

She was singing roughly every third number, and her throat was beginning to notice the unaccustomed exercise. When Jenny approached the piano and suggested she take a break, she agreed gratefully. "Max says the customers would keep you here all night, Miss Hyatt," Jenny said in her quiet voice. "You're very good."

Samantha ignored the reference to Max. "Thank you, Jenny. Our introduction was rather offhand but I hope you'll call me Sam." She warmed toward this quiet girl. Jenny was only conventionally pretty, nothing like the flamboyant comeliness of her sister. "Is your name 'Howard,' too?" she asked.

Jenny held out her left hand to display the narrow gold band with a proud smile. "Oh, no. I'm married. My husband is Johnny Worley. You've met him." When Samantha looked blank Jenny prompted, "Johnny and the Rural Route."

Samantha was delighted. "I don't think he ever told me his last name. Johnny is the one who sent me here."

"I know," said Jenny. "He was really sorry he couldn't use you himself."

Samantha made a face. "I wasn't good enough."

"Johnny said you were too good."

And whatever Johnny said was gospel, thought Samantha, almost smiling at the worshipful way the young woman spoke of her husband. The ring was very shiny. "How long have you been married?" she asked.

"Three months." Jenny could still blush.

Samantha wondered if she had ever been that naive. The word made her pause, remembering the man who had called her that a short while ago. And then called her other things. Her eyes went involuntarily to the bar to find him watching Jenny with a fierce protective glare. Did he think she would say anything to hurt this gentle creature? Yes, he probably did think that and with good reason. Inexplicable tears burned behind her eyes. "Jenny, is there any place I could go to be alone for a few minutes?" She hated the huskiness in her voice.

Immediately Jenny was all concern. "Are you ill? Let's go to the office."

"No!" She hadn't meant to speak so harshly.

Jenny gave her a strange look.

"Is there someplace else?" she asked quietly.

Jenny thought for a moment. "Yes. Come on. I'll take you."

IT WAS ALMOST nine o'clock and Samantha felt as if she'd been playing the piano for days instead of hours when Mr. Townsend walked in. He waved and took a seat at the bar.

She finished the tune she was playing and immediately switched to one of the songs he'd requested during her audition. He lifted his glass to her in a silent toast, which she acknowledged with a smile.

The lounge was nearly empty now; only a few stalwarts remained, and of those, only one or two were slightly tipsy.

Max propped his elbows on the bar beside Mr. Townsend, building a tower with his fingers on which to rest his chin. The two men carried on a long low conversation.

Samantha wondered what they were talking about. Was Max telling his boss that the new pianist was a cold snobbish bitch? While she watched, he straightened and gave his employer a consoling smile, shaking his head. That was certainly strange. Why would Max be offering solace to the man he worked for?

Samantha frowned, dismissing both of them from her thoughts, and went into her new employer's special favorite, "Smoke Gets in Your Eyes." She must have misread his expression, but at the moment she was too tired and her throat hurt too much to speculate any further about Max Stanwood.

She was closing everything up for the night when both men approached the piano. "Max tells me that your performance went over very well with the customers tonight, Samantha," said Mr. Townsend.

Her eyes sought Max's. Had he decided to forgive her for the disparaging remark? But his expression told her nothing. "Thank you," she said with quiet sincerity. She smiled at Mr. Townsend but her answer was for Max.

"My wife sends her apologies for missing your first night here. She was... with our grandchild tonight." He flicked a glance at Max. "But she's looking forward to hearing you play tomorrow."

"And I'm looking forward to meeting her," Samantha murmured politely.

"Thank you, too, for remembering my favorite song, Samantha. Good night. Good night, Max."

"Good night, Abe. See you tomorrow."

The older man left. His shoulders were not as square as they had been on Wednesday and he looked tired. Samantha wondered if the grandchild he'd spoken of was ill.

Abe? Max and his employer were certainly on familiar terms. Well, it was none of her business. She fumbled under the bench for her purse.

"Sam...." Max slid onto the bench beside her. His shoulder brushed against hers and she tried to control her sudden shiver at his nearness. "I was rough on you. I'm sorry," he said quietly. Simple words, but like the sweetest song she'd ever heard.

"We got off to a bad start," he continued. "Can we begin again?"

She continued to stare at the purse in her hands, playing with the silver clasp. She wanted to apologize to him too, but she hesitated, not sure how to word it without sounding condescending again.

He covered her hands with his to still their movement. "Can't you even look at me?"

"Not until I apologize, but I'm not sure what to say," she blurted.

"You mean you're speechless?" he asked gently. She noted the amusement in his voice with a feeling of relief that she would have to examine later.

She lifted her eyes to his. "I'm sorry, too, Max. I...."

One finger on her lips halted further words. "That's enough. You don't have to say anything more."

"You forgive too easily."

He smiled that wonderful tender smile she'd seen when she opened her eyes to find this man in her line of vision for the first time. His fingers trailed across her cheek to tuck a strand of hair behind her ear, and lingered. "I have an idea that it will be difficult to stay mad at you for very long." He stood and reached for her hand. "Are you as hungry as I am?"

Samantha hesitated only briefly, then scrambled out after him. "I'm starved. Are we going to eat?" she asked, laughing.

He grinned as he divested himself of the apron and tossed it onto the bar. "Are we going to eat? Lady, you don't know the half of it!"

"MAX, I CANNOT HOLD another bite!" Samantha leaned back against the padded seat and shook her head at the platter he held out to her. There was already a high pile of shrimp shells on her plate.

He grinned and helped himself to more of the pink jumbos.

They were sitting on the railed wooden porch of a downtown seaside restaurant. The tide was low and a broad expanse of white sand was bleached silver by the moonlight; the sounds of the surf were muffled by distance. Only one other party shared the services of the lone waitress and they had opted for a table indoors, leaving the porch to Samantha and Max.

Max had his back to the view while she was facing it. The juice dripped down his hands as he peeled another shrimp, dipped it into bright red sauce and popped it into his mouth. "Umm. I have an idea. Why don't you peel and I'll eat?"

"Why don't you peel several at once?" She laughed. "Then you'd be prepared." A wayward breeze picked up a strand of her hair and whipped it across her eyes. She pushed it aside.

"Oh, no. That's the way *you* do it. I'm a peel-and-eat sort. Take my pleasure as it comes and don't ask questions. *You* can be the Boy Scout," he offered magnanimously.

She looked up at him, a question in her eyes. Was that how he saw her? A cautious person? Afraid to take chances? Always prepared? Well, admittedly, that was how she used to be. But she wasn't that way anymore...was she? When she'd moved to Destin it was with the intention of changing her life-style completely, of loosening the demands of a high-pressure career. She had thought she'd succeeded, but now she wasn't so sure.

Max's attention was on the shrimp and she took the opportunity to study him. Aside from his obvious good looks, he was a man who seemed to radiate calm acceptance of his place in life. But there was still something that teased her about him, a hint of hidden force, strength of character and tolerance, which didn't quite jell with his choice of profession.

Max's own reflections were following a similar direction. Who *was* this enigma called Sam?

A SLIGHTLY RAISED BROW had been the only intimation of surprise when he'd followed her out of the hotel to her car two hours earlier. He hadn't asked why a piano player, anxious for a job, was driving a Mercedes. And when he'd followed her to her condominium in his own conservative sedan, he hadn't mentioned the price of real estate on Holiday Isle in Destin.

"It's a good investment," she had finally told him when she could no longer stand the suspense of his silence.

"Of course it is," he'd answered blandly as they entered her living room. "Very nice."

Her entire condo was decorated in the colors of

outdoors. She had whimsically selected the blue of the sky, the green of plants and bright yellow for the warm Florida sunshine. When she had moved, she'd sold most of her furniture, except, of course, for her huge grand piano, and one or two pieces from her mother's family. The antiques interspersed with the more contemporary divan and chairs she'd bought in Destin were an interesting contrast.

Max made a leisurely tour while she watched. "I'm impressed, Sam," he said, but there was a reserve there, as though he was withholding comment.

"Thank you. If you'll excuse me... I won't be but a minute." Samantha had caught her lip between her teeth worriedly for a moment. Then she left him among her plants while she hurriedly changed into a pair of jeans and a lavender knit top cropped off at the waist. When she returned he was idly studying the titles of the books on her shelves.

Oh, dear, she thought, but he didn't remark on the unusual choice of reading material. "Shall we go?" she asked lightly.

He turned to smile casually, too casually. But all he said was, "Certainly. You look more comfortable now."

"I am. Thanks for letting me stop by to change."

MAX WENT TO WORK on the last shrimp as the waitress appeared at his elbow. "Can I get you folks anything else?"

"Samantha? Dessert?" he asked around the bite.

"After all that? No thanks. But I would like some coffee."

He reached for a handful of paper napkins. "Make

that two. And put it in paper cups if you have them. We'll walk down to the water."

"That was delicious, Max," Samantha said a few minutes later as they ambled along the curling edge of the shore.

Max slapped a hand on his midriff and rubbed a circle there, giving a sigh of contentment. "Actually my shrimp is better. I cook it in beer."

"You can cook?" she asked in surprise.

"Careful," he warned with a half smile. "Your chauvinism is showing."

Samantha took a sip of the rapidly cooling coffee.

"I thought about cooking for you tonight," he went on. "I often use the hotel kitchen to whip something up. But I decided that if I took you to my place afterward, you might ask the same questions I'm about to ask."

Here it comes, thought Samantha. She had finally made up her mind to be open with him. Things had already progressed to the point where evasion was useless. Something was going to happen between them. It was inevitable, as she had more reason than most to know. She sighed. "You want to know where I got my money."

"Your money?" He sounded genuinely surprised, but she wasn't fooled. She knew that he had to be curious.

"Why would I want to know that? It's none of my business where you got it."

Her disbelief must have shown in her face, because he gave her a teasing grin. "Unless you stole it. Did you?"

"Of course not!"

"Prostitution? Selling drugs?"

"Max!" She stopped walking and shot him a look of indignation. "That isn't funny. I got my money in a perfectly legitimate way."

"Good. Then let's forget your money." He reached for her hand and tugged, but when they resumed their pace he didn't let go. "What I do want to know is...." Suddenly he seemed unsure. His footsteps paused and he kicked at the sand, then moved forward again. As though he'd come to a decision, he took the coffee from her unresisting fingers and emptied the contents of both containers onto the sand. He crushed the paper cups easily and jammed them in the back pocket of his jeans.

Samantha waited for whatever was coming, apprehension spiced with anticipation churning inside her.

Max faced her squarely and took her shoulders in his hands. "What I want to know is how you felt about me.... What was your reaction the first time we looked at each other?" He let out his breath. "What did you feel, Sam?" he added quietly.

She smiled, knowing this was important. "The Awakening of Romantic Hope."

Max chuckled, a totally masculine, totally satisfied sound, not realizing that she had spoken in capitals. "I felt the same way, darlin'," he admitted. Relief softened his voice as he pulled her into his arms. "But I couldn't put it quite so poetically."

"Well, I ought to be able to," she said, resigned to her confession. "I wrote the book."

3

"You certainly did," Max murmured into her ear. His breath was delightfully warm. He nuzzled down to the sensitive spot on her neck where a pulse throbbed heavily.

It absolutely amazed her, when she had the presence of mind to think, that her body responded so readily to his touch. She'd better get this said before she completely forgot what they were talking about. "I mean literally, Max."

"I do, too, sweetheart. I've wanted you like hell from the moment I first looked into those golden eyes."

"Max!" she pleaded weakly, pushing at the hair that whipped into her eyes. "Stop nibbling on me and listen."

"But you taste so good." He smiled against her skin, using his mustache to tickle under her chin. "Okay, okay. I'll behave." He sighed and raised his head. "This would work better if we were sitting down anyway. Without your high-heeled shoes you're so little...." He cocked his head to one side and grinned to let her know that he really didn't mind and linked his hands loosely together behind her back.

Her palms were flat against his chest. She felt the strong beat of his heart under her fingers and wondered at the warmth of his skin through the shirt, before sternly returning her attention to the problem at hand. "Max, I wrote a book about this very thing."

"You're a writer?" He seemed pleased at the idea.

"No. I'm... was... am a psychologist. The name of the book is *Psychology for Today's Life-style.* It's a guide for counselors."

"A psychologist." He worried over the word, pronouncing it very slowly as though examining it with his tongue before thinking about it.

Samantha held her breath. She'd had all kinds of responses from men upon learning her profession. Most of them were predictable: they either thought she could solve all their problems, or they were completely intimidated. A lot of promising relationships had been cut short by the revelation that she was a psychologist. With Max, she didn't know what to expect.

"I don't think I've heard of the book," he said slowly.

"You probably haven't. It was written for the profession rather than the general public."

He was quiet for a long moment, frowning distractedly. Then the frown changed to one of indignation. He dropped his hands from her waist. "Then would you mind explaining what the hell you're doing playing piano in a bar?"

"Music has always been my first love. I, uh, I had a chance to make a change in my life. So I decided to see if I could make a living at it."

"Why would you have wanted to make a change?"

She'd been afraid that would be his next question.

Her chin went up. "That's none of your business," she told him sharply.

He scowled at her skeptically and turned on his heel, striding back toward the stream of light that poured from the restaurant. With his long legs it was only a second before he was yards away.

Samantha scooted to catch up with him, hoping to neutralize his resentment. "Max, slow down," she begged. "I wasn't being deceptive. I really wanted to return to music. That's why. Max! Please...."

He suddenly halted and she crashed into the back of him. He turned and put out his hands to steady her. "That first day, all that crap about bartenders being psychologists. You were putting me on, weren't you?" he charged angrily.

"No, I—"

"Don't lie to me, Samantha!" The hands on her shoulders gave her a small shake.

"I'm not lying!" she retorted. "If anyone was putting on anybody, it was you. Standing there, not saying a word, just wiping...and wiping...." She threw up her hands. "And that counter was perfectly clean. I don't see how you have the nerve to accuse me of putting you on."

His lips curved into an unpleasant smile. "So it bothered you, did it?"

"No! It didn't bother me," she denied with heat. She planted her fists on her hips and glared up at him with a stubborn thrust to her jaw. "After all, *I* was the one who knew what was going on."

"Going on?" His antagonism faded in the face of hers and his voice was dangerously low, but Samantha ignored the warning inside her that said to go slow.

"Going on between us. The—" Uh-oh. She took a breath. "The—" she flapped her hand at him "—you know," she said, more quietly.

"'The Awakening of Romantic Hope'?" A wayward breeze whipped his hair forward over his brow and he raked it away. "Is that what you mean?"

So he hadn't missed that. And he was going to make her say it, damn him. Glossing over facts with polite little phrases wasn't his way. "Yes." Her voice was just a whisper now.

"Sam, come here. No, don't fight me." He wrapped her in a firm embrace and rested his chin on the top of her head. "Did you think that you were the only one who knew what was happening between us?" he asked softly.

His voice was a rumble above her or she probably wouldn't have heard him over the sound of the waves hitting the beach. She shook her head, grateful for his warmth, grateful that he no longer seemed angry.

"Do you think I needed a book to tell me that you were the most beautiful, the most desirable, the sexiest woman I'd ever seen?"

She tried to rationalize the pleasure that coursed through her at his words. "But I knew what it all meant, what was going to happen. That's why I was so nasty. I guess I was worried. I really hadn't planned to let myself become involved with anyone right now." She snuggled her cheek closer and sighed contentedly. "I of all people should have realized that it was inevitable."

"Are you trying to tell me, darlin', that this was meant to be?"

She nodded. "Stage One, anyway," she explained languorously. It felt so good to be held like this. His hands were trailing up and down her back in a sensual massage. If they went just a little bit farther down she would feel them on the bare skin beneath the top.

Suddenly she was thrust away from that heavenly warmth as Max took her hand and proceeded toward the restaurant.

"Max! What...?" She stumbled in his wake.

"Come on. We're going to have another cup of coffee and you're going to tell me all about Stage One."

AN HOUR LATER Max set down his mug, empty of the third refill, and shook his head in frustration. What did she have anyway, he asked himself, that other women didn't have? Without a doubt she was a fabulous creature, but she wasn't the first of those he'd known. Why was he so excited? For that was certainly the word—he felt excitement every time he looked at her, every time he caught a whiff of her scent, hell, every time he even thought of her.

That kiss they'd shared in the office had ignited fires that he'd thought were forever extinguished. Dammit! He wasn't an adolescent! But he'd come very close to losing control of his libido. When she moved against him in that hungry little way, he'd wanted to take her that minute, on the floor if necessary, and hang the consequences. Such a loss of control was completely foreign to him.

He leaned back in the wooden chair until the press of the slats against his back was almost painful, then shoved his hands into his pockets, making an effort to keep his attention on what she was saying.

The excitement wasn't only sexual, either. He barely knew her and yet she was the first woman who had ever stimulated a real longing in him for home and hearth, for a family, for children. The feeling had been sudden, unexpected and unexplainable. Sure, he'd thought about marriage. He'd even been engaged once. Sensitive feelings made him shy away from those memories. But they had been purposeful decisions made with his head, rather than this emotional declaration coming from his heart.

She was a maddening little thing, and a psychologist besides! He listened to her elaborate on how she had begun her research, written the book in hopes of contributing something of value to help battle the rising divorce rate. She certainly felt strongly about the subject. There was a certain intense sincerity in her face when she spoke of it. She was either divorced herself or her parents had been.

She cupped her chin in her hand and leaned forward. A long strand of hair hesitated on her shoulder for a minute, then swung free to dangle in front of her breast. His fingers itched to bury themselves in that glorious mass, to see it spread across his pillow.

With a superhuman effort he sent his thoughts veering off in another direction. There was a further incongruity. She was so tiny. Because of his size he'd always been drawn to tall women. He felt more comfortable with them. Not that he felt uncomfortable with petite Samantha—on the contrary, his pleasure in her company was part of the puzzle. He was totally comfortable and happy when he was in her presence, even when she had that saucy little nose in the air, even when she was raving at him, and even when that practical streak vexed him to near distraction.

"You'll forgive me, Dr. Hyatt, if I tell you that all this sounds very clinical. There's nothing at all romantic about it."

"You're not *trying* to understand, Max." Her frustration seemed as strong as his. "What I'm saying is that emotional honesty is much more fulfilling in the long run than emotional sloppiness."

"Emotional sloppiness?" He tried to hide a grin.

Samantha glared at him. "And it's also much less dangerous in a relationship," she said with a touch of fierceness.

His dubious brow went up another notch. "Tell me again what will happen in Stage One." He didn't really give a damn about hearing the dry facts again. He simply wanted to sit here longer, to watch her, to listen to that sexy voice. He could listen all night.

"I've already told you." She shrugged and relaxed against the chair back. "Well, okay. One more time. Then I have to go home. It's after midnight, Max. My throat was sore from singing when we left the hotel. Now it's really raw and I'm tired," she complained.

He picked up her hand where it rested on the table between them and laced their fingers together. "I'm sorry, darlin'. I just want to be sure I comprehend all you're saying." Her hands were so small that her fingers barely reached across his knuckles. And her skin was like silk, smooth and cool. He made a pocket with his other hand over hers. "Are you cold?"

She met his eyes with a blank stare that seemed to

ask *Are you crazy?* and he almost laughed aloud. "No," she finally answered. "I'm fine." The pink tip of her tongue came out to moisten her upper lip.

It was an unconscious act, but its effect on him was instantaneous. God, he wanted her! If her hands were this soft, what was the rest of her like? Her breasts? Her stomach? The skin on the inside of her thighs was probably like luxurious satin. He groaned.

"Did you say something?" she asked.

It would scare the daylights out of her if she could see into his mind right now. "No," he said too harshly. "Go on. I'm listening."

He squirmed in his seat, trying to ease the sudden painful restriction of his jeans. *Think about something else,* he commanded himself in desperation. Did the Braves have a chance in the pennant race this year? The young pitcher from Saint Louis should help. However, if a strong home-run hitter didn't materialize soon, they could kiss their chances goodbye. Gradually, with a superhuman effort, he brought his raging desire under control, until finally he drew a long heavy breath of relief.

SAMANTHA SPOKE in her best lecturing tone, trying to ignore the trail of fire traveling up her arm from his caressing thumb. The heat spread through her heart straight to her midsection. It was setting in motion all sorts of feelings preliminary to making love. Though those feelings were natural and normal she didn't feel able to cope with them tonight. She willed her thoughts to remain on the subject.

"Stage One in the natural progression of a romance is when two people are instantly aware of each other. Some of my colleagues refer to it as the 'love zap' theory." She made a face and Max interrupted.

"You didn't mention that before."

"Didn't I?" She shrugged. "It's the same thing as the old 'love at first sight' idea," she explained, and he nodded sagely.

"You'd be surprised at the number of couples who take that for Everlasting Love and immediately run off and get married or move in together."

Max tried but didn't quite succeed in hiding his smile.

"Do you think it's funny? Well, don't! Do you know that at least half of the marriages in this country end in divorce? And even if couples do not choose the commitment of marriage, most people are just as deeply hurt when a love affair breaks up. It's a devastating experience."

Max stood up, and placing one hand on the table and one on the chair behind her head, leaned down to give her a soft unhurried kiss. But the amusement was still in his voice and his eyes when he spoke again. "I wasn't smiling about that, darlin'. I was thinking of how much fun this is going to be. You're way ahead of me. I suppose I'd better read your book, because I hadn't even reached the point of our moving in together, much less marriage."

Samantha's eyes grew wide. "I didn't mean... you weren't... oh, for heaven's sake!" she sputtered.

He was laughing in earnest now and the sound was rich and deep, like a warm cloak that spread over her. He took her shoulders in his big hands and brought her to her feet.

Reluctantly she met his grin. "I didn't mean to

sound like you didn't stand a chance, Max. I'm not looking for a commitment at all."

"Oh, Dr. Hyatt." He chuckled and gathered her against the warmth of his chest. "I haven't stood a chance since the moment I first saw you. My Romantic Hope is fully awake." He let her go only long enough to pick up the check and then guided her with an arm across her shoulders to the cashier's desk.

Digging into the pocket of his jeans he came out with some crumpled bills. Their waitress was also the cashier. "Y'all come back," she said cheerfully.

The parking lot was paved with broken oyster shells, and even in her sneakers Samantha was unsteady as she walked. But she wasn't sure whether her wobble was due to the uneven surface or to Max's proprietary hold.

"YOU DON'T HAVE TO COME UP with me," Samantha said when Max parked the car and turned off the ignition. She was beginning to feel nervous. All the way home from the restaurant Max had held on to her hand. On more than one occasion he raised it to kiss her wrist or her fingers with tender brushes of his lips, and his glances were filled with transparent anticipation. He seemed to have the impression that everything had been said that needed to be said. But it hadn't—not by a long shot. All she had to do was convince him of that.

Now he smiled and his eyes darkened to a seductive glow. "I want to," he said huskily, opening the door on his side. When he came around to help her out, he handled her as though she were a fragile bit of crystal. "And you want me to, don't you?"

She sighed when he linked their fingers together. "You know, Max, I think you're right."

"Of course I am, darlin'." He gave her fingers a light squeeze.

Her head came up with a jerk. "I don't mean about that." Lengthening her stride, she tried to move ahead of him, but he refused to release her hand, so she found herself in the awkward position of pulling him along behind her. She didn't speak again until they had transversed the lobby, deserted except for the night watchman, and reached the elevator. She jabbed the Up button with a free finger. "You should read my book. These things don't happen *this* fast."

The brushed steel doors slid silently apart and they stepped inside. Max pushed the button this time and then turned to her. His head tilted endearingly to one side and a brow arched the question before he could voice it. "They don't?"

Damn! If only he wasn't so handsome! But looks didn't matter all that much in Stage One, she reminded herself. It was that indefinable something called "chemistry." He could have ears large enough to fly with, she thought as she looked at the flat, well-shaped appendages, and still the electricity would have been there. She was reminded of some of the incongruous couples she had worked with. "No. Stage One might be the end of it." She shrugged.

He tugged her closer, his free hand burrowing under her hair, and gave her a brief smiling kiss on the end of her nose. "Samantha, I can assure you, there's not the remotest possibility of this being the end."

Before she could correct his assumption, the doors opened again. He followed her down the carpeted hallway. She hadn't taken a purse with her and now she held out her hand for her key; but instead of giving it to her he took it from his pocket and fitted it into the lock.

Samantha steeled herself for an argument—he seemed to be ready to discuss the issue further and there was no way she could talk anymore tonight. She stepped into the opening and turned to face him. "I enjoyed dinner, Max. Thank you."

The perfect gentleman before her held out her key and said, "It was my pleasure."

She took the tiny bit of metal, warm from his body heat, wrapped it in her fist and looked up at him. "Well, uh, good night," she mumbled. But she hesitated at the threshold. "We...you could..." she stammered. Why was it that one look from those blue eyes and she couldn't manage to make a coherent sentence?

"Are you trying to say that I can kiss you good night?" Max asked with a gleam of amusement in his eyes.

"If you'd like to," she answered softly. They really should, she rationalized. The only way they were going to discover whether or not there was a relationship developing was to try a few of these things.

"I'd like to, very much." As he spoke Max swiveled her until she rested against the door facing. Very slowly he brought his long body in contact with hers; but they didn't fit at all. His thighs ended somewhere around her belly button and her head as she looked up at him was bent at an uncomfortable angle.

Helplessly Samantha began to laugh. "You see—" she grinned "—it's a thing such as this that can kill off Stage One before it begins."

"Uh-uh," he said, shaking his head confidently. "It'll take more than this to kill off *our* Stage One, darlin'. Come here." Powerful arms wrapped around her waist and lifted her easily, bringing their faces to a level.

What the heck. Samantha circled his neck with her arms and grinned wider. "That's what I like, a man who can improvise."

Slowly his smile began to fade as they both became aware of the convergence of their bodies. Their banter was forgotten in the tangible excitement and heat building between them, fusing flesh to flesh despite their clothing. His growing arousal met the eager softness of her thighs as she moved her legs slightly, conceding the need in both of them for more intimate contact.

A soft moan escaped from one throat to be countered by a gasp from the other. Who moaned; who gasped? Neither knew; neither cared. Reality and reason were abandoned as their bodies shifted, melded and shifted again.

Max's mustache nudged the corner of her lips. He mouthed a hungry path across them and back, leaving a moist trail of unfulfilled yearning. "You taste so good," he whispered along the way. "Your mouth is so sweet... and warm... like honey."

Samantha's lashes drifted down to partially screen her eyes, while her lips parted further, admitting his soft words, his heated breath. His tongue teased underneath her upper lip, sending a delightfully unfamiliar flutter down her spine, and then dipped deeper into her mouth to find the tip of her own.

The tiny lick was a magnetic lure, drawing her tongue forward to follow his in an erotic exploration that sent her senses on a whirling sparkling spin through a world of star-filled galaxies. Her fingers combed through the thick silky strands of his hair.

One of his hands climbed her spine, burrowing under the curtain of loose auburn curls at her nape. He lifted his head a fraction of an inch to look deeply into her half-open eyes. "Kiss me, Samantha!" It was a whispered groan. "Kiss me!"

The hands in his hair gave up their tactile quest and her arms wound around his neck tightly. She tilted her head and her soft lips moved over his, hungry and evocative, exhilarated by his desire, nourishing it with her own; until finally in self-protection she had to end the kiss, or she would be begging him to make love to her. She buried her flushed face in his neck.

He was breathing as heavily as she was. His hand moved up and down her back restlessly, in a ridiculously extravagant attempt to soothe her.

She smiled against the skin of his throat. This was definitely a relationship that offered the possibility of a future. "Max," she sighed.

He raised his head. His eyes were unfocused, glazed. Slowly he loosened his grip and let her slide down his hard length. The toes of her sneakers touched the floor, but he didn't let go. His shoulders hunched protectively over her and his lips found the pulse beat at her temple. "What happens in Stage Two?" he groaned into her hair.

Samantha's voice was more gravelly than usual. "We haven't finished with One."

"I'm not sure I'll survive." His hands clenched into the cloth covering her back, then eased. They took a firm grip on her shoulders and he stepped back, letting his eyes wander hungrily over her tangled hair, her swollen lips, her breasts, heaving slightly under the knit top. His lips curved in a rueful smile. "I'm not sure you will, either."

"I know," she breathed.

"Well, then...?"

Samantha's hands came up quickly to hold him away. "Not yet, Max."

"When?" he asked bluntly, spreading his hands. "This whole thing has happened in double time. Dammit! I want you. You want me. We're both mature adults. What's the point in waiting?"

It was the sexual frustration talking, she knew that, but she wouldn't be pushed. She didn't even want this, she reminded herself. A love affair was the last thing she needed, so her reaction took the form of annoyance. "It's too dangerous," she snapped. "Don't you see? I don't want to hurt you, or to be hurt myself. If we take it any further at all, we must take it slowly...in stages!"

Max gave a deep sigh and, keeping his feet in place, let himself fall backward. It wasn't a great distance but his hips hit the opposite side of the doorframe with a visible jolt. He jammed his hands into the pockets of his jeans and frowned. After a minute he spoke. "Okay, Sam," he said in a low voice. "I'll give you time, but go get the damned book. I'm going to read it, too!"

Samantha looked at him dubiously. "Are you sure? It's rather specialized. You might...."

His face was a terrible thing to see when he was really angry. The blue eyes spit ice. His jaw firmed angrily, and a furious red color came up from his throat to stain his skin. "Dr. Hyatt," he said tightly. "I may be just a bartender, but I am not stupid!"

In a way she was grateful for his anger. His everlasting patience with her was just too good to be true. Anger made him more human and she could react to it honestly and in kind.

Levering herself away from the door, she swung toward the bookshelves. "That wasn't what I meant!" She stalked across the floor waving her hand for punctuation. "The only copies I have are extremely technical ones. Another edition was written for interested laymen, like lawyers, doctors, ministers and anyone else who could use the information in a professional way." She jerked a volume from its spot and marched back to him. "But be my guest, Einstein!" She slammed the book on his midriff and took great delight in seeing him wince. "I simply thought you might enjoy the other edition more. You wouldn't have to wade through the jargon." She braced one arm on the edge of the door, ready to slam it in his face, and the other arm on her hip. "Good night, Mr. Stanwood," she said coldly.

Max had automatically closed his hands around the book. "Sam...." He put out a hand to stop the motion of the door. "Sam, can you deny that the idea of my being a bartender bothers you?" he asked quietly. It was amazing. His anger had evaporated as quickly as it had flared. Something akin to disappointment seemed to have taken its place.

Samantha deflated like a balloon. "Max, sometimes attraction between two people is a result of the things they have in common. But sometimes it happens because one of them is seeking something entirely different from what they have known. Does that make sense?" When he nodded, she continued. "I've never known a bartender before. You're different, and maybe that's your appeal. I came to Destin seeking a change." Her slender shoulders lifted and fell in a shrug of confusion. "But I like you." She sighed. "All I can say is that we have to know each other a lot better before I can answer your question."

"You don't pull your punches, do you?" His

mouth twisted in a regretful grin and he dropped his hand from the door.

She folded her arms across her chest and took up the relaxed stance against the frame again, studying her toes. "I know I'm too practical," she admitted. "I don't want to be insulting, but I don't want to be less than honest with you, either."

"Why did you come to Destin, Samantha? What was so wrong with your life that you had to change it so drastically? Was it a man?"

Her hesitation lasted for only a moment. What could it hurt? He might as well know. "Two of them," she told him bitterly.

"Two?" His expressive brow lifted.

"I thought I was in love with one of them. The other one was my father."

"Let's take them one at a time," he said gently. He propped his shoulders against the doorframe in a stance that told her he was prepared to stay all night if necessary.

"If we're going to get into this you might as well come inside," she said and led the way.

Max closed the door behind them.

Samantha waved him to a seat. "Do you want more coffee or anything?"

The twinkle in the blue eyes warned her that the question was dangerous, but mercifully he didn't comment. She was too tired to play word games and he seemed to sense it.

"No, I'm going in a minute." He lowered himself onto her sofa and stretched both arms along its back. "Don't you want to sit down?"

She perched on one end of the piano stool. Trying to keep her voice on its normally sensible level, she said, "I was engaged to an eminently suitable man, another psychologist, my boss as a matter of fact. About a year ago I discovered that we didn't have as much in common as I thought. His idea of a happy marriage and mine didn't mesh at all. And that is all I'm going to say about him," she said stubbornly.

"Fine," agreed Max with more aplomb than she expected. "What about your father?"

"My father," she sighed. "My father was destroyed by love. I've had enough training to rationally understand why but I still can't understand emotionally. When my mother left I was eleven. He blamed me for her defection, but he also became dependent on me. Even after I was grown and moved away I had to go by to see him every day or he had fits." She shook her head sadly and looked across at him. "There you have the reason for my research." She tried to smile but didn't quite succeed. Her eyes felt pinched around the edges.

Max studied her face for a minute. Then he slapped the cushion of the sofa and stood, stretching his long body. "Well," he said, plunging his hands into the pockets of his jeans. "I'd better be going." He came to stand in front of her.

All of a sudden she wanted to explain further. It was important, though she didn't know why, that he have the whole story. She opened her mouth to speak.

A long finger lifted her chin. There was an expression in his eyes that was totally unreadable, but at least he smiled on the surface. "No more tonight. You're exhausted. We have plenty of time to learn about each other."

"Will we?" she asked huskily. She didn't want to

She blinked rapidly to clear her eyes, remembering. Divorce was a subject that she felt intensely about.

She whipped over onto her stomach and buried her face in the pillow. Even the therapy that had been mandatory for her degree in psychology hadn't been able to wipe out the pain and rejection of being a wishbone child. Her mother and father had used her to get back at each other from the time she was eleven, when they had split her world in half.

The seesaw battle for custody had not ended until her mother's death, when Samantha was fourteen. And then the situation had simply gotten worse. With his adversary gone her father had simply turned all his attention to his only child. And his love had become the smothering type.

Throwing off the covers, Samantha got out of bed and went onto the balcony, hoping the ocean breezes would blow those memories away. *Think about something else,* she told herself sternly, propping her elbows on the iron railing.

The moon was out of sight behind the building, but its glow paved the restless water below with silver pathways. The soft sighs of the waves as they gently brushed the shore usually served to soothe her into sleep. But tonight, as tired as she was, she had never felt so wide awake.

Samantha recognized her problem. It had been an emotionally charged day. A new, completely different job, and a new, completely different man, she thought, finally succumbing to the inevitability of readmitting Max into her reflections.

She'd kept him out for—how long?—ten minutes?

admit, even to herself, how much the promise warmed her.

He nodded decisively and caught her hand to take her to the door with him. "We most definitely will." He reached for the knob. "I suppose if you can venture into Stage One with a bartender, I can venture in with the bar's piano player. Good night, darlin'." He gave her a little push and closed the door between them.

What a strange thing for him to say, thought Samantha as she fit the chain into its slot and turned the key in the dead-bolt lock.

An hour later she was still mulling over his words. She lay on her back with her hands loosely linked together over her stomach and stared at the play of light and shadow on the ceiling.

The draperies were open to their fullest, and she had left the sliding glass door open a crack, hoping the sounds of the sea would lull her into sleep. But her eyes were wide and her brain refused to shut down for the night.

She wondered if Max was reading. Probably not. A page or two of a clinical psychologist's dissection of the modern-day love affair would bore anyone stiff. She remembered when the Masters and Johnson study was published. Everyone rushed out to buy the book, thinking they were going to read something really spicy, but the technical aspects soon discouraged the general public.

Of course, Masters and Johnson had studied sexual habits and deviations. Samantha's book centered on the emotional aspects of love, dealing with the anticipation of long-term commitment in the hope of helping stem the rising tide of divorce.

Her body began its signals in instant reaction to the vivid picture of him that her mind eagerly provided, perhaps in a subconscious effort to chase the unhappier thoughts away.

She smiled and knew that the smile was slightly feline, almost hungry, knew that her pupils were beginning to dilate. Her throat had a dry feel to it, causing an involuntary swallow. There was a prickling in her nipples and a heavy throb between her thighs, as though blood were rushing in to nourish a need. These symptoms were an indication of the intensity of her desire for Max Stanwood.

Stage One had never solidified so quickly for her before. She had sparkled and encouraged and flirted with men in this stage, but she had not felt the physical response as strongly as this. Until the Possibility of Linking Life-styles occurred, the physical reaction was usually much tamer. She would have to watch herself. It was often easy to add dangerous excitement to a first stage by becoming attracted to, and infatuated by, someone whose flaws were obvious.

Max Stanwood. What did "Max" stand for? Maximilian? She frowned. He had certainly been angry with her over the book. She *had* been condescending that first day, she admitted, squirming mentally. But why was he defensive about his job? His capabilities? If he felt that way why didn't he do something else? He seemed intelligent. She didn't think bartending could be much of a challenge.

Maybe he'd had a learning disability as a child. Max must be thirty-three or thirty-four. Only recently had the movers and shakers in education realized that a great many bright children had difficulties in school stemming from physical rather than mental problems. He would have been long out of school before the recent progress made in that field could have helped him.

If that was so, she could help him, she decided happily. Lifting her hands high above her head she stretched her body lazily and gave a wide yawn. She made a mental note to send for some books on the subject, and went back inside to climb into bed. She was asleep as soon as her head touched the pillow.

SAMANTHA WAS HUMMING around a mouthful of toothpaste when she heard the telephone. Grabbing a towel, she hurried into her bedroom.

"Good morning," Max's cheerful voice greeted her.

She grinned crazily at the wall and wiped the last smidgen of mint-flavored foam from her chin. "Good morning."

"Were you awake?"

The digital clock on the bedside table informed her that it was seven fifty-seven. "I've been up for hours," she said gently.

He groaned. "Now that may be a real hurdle to our reaching Stage Two. Don't tell me you're one of those dedicated morning people."

Samantha perched on the edge of the rumpled bed and stretched her bare legs in front of her, toes curling into the plush carpet. One finger twisted into the spiral cord. "As a matter of fact, I just got up," she admitted.

"Let's go out for breakfast," Max suggested. His voice lowered slightly. "I sure as hell can't wait until four o'clock to get on with Stage One. Can you?"

Her husky laugh was met with his rather choked one. "No," she said softly. "Why don't you come over here and I'll cook breakfast?"

"Right now?"

His eagerness came over the wires at her like a jolt of electricity. She had to take a moment to catch her breath. "Give me half an hour. I was just about to get into the shower."

It was his turn to be silent. "Dr. Hyatt, did your extensive training instruct you in the art of subtle torture?" he asked in a very low voice. "Do you know what the pictures I envision are doing to me right now?"

"Max, please...." It was a whispered plea.

"I can see the warm water splashing on your shoulders, trailing down between your breasts to—"

"Half an hour," she interrupted frantically and hung up. She covered her burning cheeks with shaking hands. How could she ever resist him long enough for them to get to know each other, when her passionate response was as immediate and powerful as his?

The smell of bacon frying mingled with freshly perked coffee when, exactly thirty minutes later, the doorbell rang and rang and rang.

"I'm coming. All right, I'm coming!" Samantha called as she hurried to the door. She tucked her lavender blouse more securely into the waistband of the matching shorts and pushed the mane of auburn hair away from her face, flushed from the heat of the stove. "Your impatience is—Max! What on earth?"

He was ringing the bell with an elbow while juggling several packages and a huge armful of flowers.

"Let me help." She reached forward to take something.

"No. If you pull out anything the whole load will go." He brushed past her, grinning. "You should never have given me thirty minutes to kill."

He deposited everything on the bar that separated the kitchen from the living-dining area, and turned to lift her off her feet, whirling her around in an exuberant hug. He gave her a loud smacking kiss and set her on her bare feet. "You look beautiful," he told her enthusiastically.

Then he turned to his bounty, rubbing his hands together in anticipation. "It smells great in here! Bacon, coffee. I'm starving. But first...." He pulled a foil-wrapped bottle of champagne from one of the brown paper bags.

Samantha watched in awe. This huge vibrant man seemed to fill her apartment with zest and life. "Champagne?" she asked happily.

"Not just champagne. Mimosas!" he told her as he delved into another sack and came up with a large glass container of orange juice.

She peered around his bulk to watch him strip the foil from the bottle. "Mimosa? I've never heard of that."

"That's one of the advantages of knowing a bartender." He leered suggestively down at her. "We can come up with all manner of interesting diversions. Get me two glasses with stems." He kissed her on the forehead and the cork hit the ceiling.

Samantha jumped. "I'm not sure my crystal is safe around you." But she went into the kitchen and came up with two beautifully etched wine goblets.

"Perfect. Fine champagne deserves fine crystal.

Look at this." He turned the bottle to present the label.

"Piper Heidsieck?" she read, and then smiled an apology. "I'm afraid I don't know very much about wines, Max."

He looked horrified. "I thought *you* were the sophisticate. Actually it's much too fine a vintage to mix with anything, but what the heck? Nothing but the best for Stage One, right, darlin'?"

She crossed her arms and leaned forward on them, grinning across the counter at him. "Right!" His eyes were so blue today, his hair was combed neatly and his white shirt fairly crackled with laundry starch. As usual, the long sleeves were turned back almost to the elbows. He wore jeans, but they too had visited the laundry and emerged with a pressed crease down the legs. He looked absolutely wonderful.

Clearing his throat with an excess of dramatics he shook his head and looked at her regretfully. "Now, darlin', you can't go doing things like that to me."

Samantha looked blank. "Like what?"

His eyes dropped pointedly to her breasts and she suddenly realized that the position of her arms was pushing them together, forming a deep cleavage clearly visible in the vee of her blouse. She quickly straightened and, tugging at the hem of the shorts, murmured, "Sorry." To cover her chagrin she picked up the linens and silverware and stepped through the open door onto the balcony.

Physical awareness is never far from the surface, she thought ruefully as she spread the yellow cloth. Napkins were aligned and forks, knives and spoons spaced precisely while the happy squeals of an early-morning game on the beach registered vaguely in her brain. She looked over the railing to locate the source of the sound.

A hundred yards away a coed group of teenagers was trying to start a volleyball game. Three or four of them batted the ball back and forth across the net, but several couples stood by watching, obviously not interested in that kind of physical activity.

One couple broke away from the group to walk down to the water. The boy's arm was securely wrapped around the girl's shoulders and hers circled his waist. Their heads were close. They were oblivious to everything but each other. Samantha's mind automatically recorded Stage Two's declarations of love, and their absolute feeling that *this is the one*.

Her eyes were drawn to stare unseeingly at the horizon where the sky met the sea in two shades of blue. She tried to tell herself that only adolescents reacted to the stages of a romance with such total oblivion. But adolescents falling in love enjoyed a verve for all of life, a bubbling invigorating excitement that mature adults had learned by experience to subdue. If she and Max were lucky enough to mix the experience of maturity with the enthusiasm of youth, could they not have something very special indeed?

The answer to her question was in his warm gaze as Max stepped through the door with the two glasses in his hands. She had turned at the same moment, the railing behind her, lending support to her weakened knees.

Silently he held out one crystal goblet. The sunlight caught in a prism of the goblet's design, gilding the contents of the glass. When she accepted it with fingers that were not quite steady, he toasted her. They sipped, their eyes never breaking contact over the rims of the glasses.

The message was given and received, and now there was no hurry. No hurry at all.

The taste on her tongue was sweet and tangy, the champagne enhancing the flavor of the orange juice with a suggestion of zing. "This is very good," Samantha told him with an easy smile.

He returned the smile with one of tender perception. "I'm glad you like it."

The words didn't matter. They could have said anything. It was what they didn't say that was meaningful and important to both of them. And their thoughts didn't need to be voiced.

They turned as one. His arm circled her waist, fitting her close against his length. She felt his lips caress her temple with a touch as light as the warm breeze.

Her head lay against his shoulder in deep contentment as they stood looking out over the ocean, enjoying the sounds and smells of a beautiful new day, for a space of time that couldn't be measured by ordinary means. It was just long enough to open themselves to the vulnerability of love, just long enough to enter into Stage Two: The Future Has Begun.

5

BREAKFAST WAS A BLURRED indistinct dream. The light fruity flavor of the Mimosas blended with the more prosaic taste of bacon and eggs, neither particularly distinguishable to either Max or Samantha.

They were intoxicated—but with each other—not with the effects of champagne. Touching was compulsory. His hand covered hers briefly when she reached for the strawberry jam, and it took her a moment to recall what it was she wanted. She trailed her fingers across his shoulders when she started into the kitchen for the coffee pot. Then her arm was caught in a firm grip and she found herself sitting on his lap. The coffee was forgotten for a long moment.

Max had arranged the flowers in a pottery jug while Samantha put the food on the table, and the sweet mingling scents of roses, daisies and irises teased the two of them into deeper sensual awareness.

They were drawn magnetically forward in their chairs, their bodies leaning toward each other as they ate. The smiles on their faces were as involuntary as breathing. Smiling was a form of communication and they were communicating on every level—not only with their low murmuring voices, but also with their eyes and their body language.

Finally Max took a last swallow of coffee, gave a deep sigh and sat back against the cushion. He tossed the linen napkin on the table and glanced at the gold watch on his wrist. His fingers snaked out to interwine with hers. "I have to go," he said regretfully.

Samantha's arched brows rose. "You do?"

He nodded. "I have to work. The luncheon crowd at the pool starts warming up about eleven and the piano bar opens at four."

She nodded too, not overly disturbed by his announcement. The short separation would only make their reunion that much sweeter when they met later in the bar. And tonight...they both knew what would probably happen tonight. If not tonight, they would make love soon. But Samantha didn't feel pressured. She knew that Max wouldn't rush her if she wasn't ready.

Max looked over the railing to the crowds that had begun to gather on the beach. "Come inside with me," he murmured huskily. He got to his feet and tugged on her hand. "I want a kiss to live on until I see you again."

She skirted the table and went under his arm as though it was a longtime habit. "You make it seem as if it will be for days instead of hours," she teased unsteadily.

"That's the way I'll feel, darlin', because I've only recently found you," he replied with simple sincerity. Just before they passed through the door he reached over to take a yellow rose from the bouquet. He lifted it to his nose to test the scent and then trailed the blossom slowly across her chin.

Samantha inhaled deeply of the heady perfume. It

was a sweetly romantic thing to do and she smiled slightly; her heavy lashes sank to her cheeks. "The flowers are beautiful. Thank you," she murmured.

"Not as beautiful as you are. Oh, Samantha, you are a miracle," he whispered as he turned her into his arms. "You smell like heaven, feel so good in my arms."

His embrace was constrictive, threatening her delicate bone structure; but his lips were almost hesitant in their movement over hers.

Impatiently Samantha arched closer, reaching up and tangling her fingers in his hair, trying to deepen the kiss. She closed her eyes to savor the kaleidoscope of color behind her lids.

He gave a low moan and wrenched his mouth away to bury his face against her hair. He took a long shuddering breath. "Sam, Sam, darlin', please...I want you so badly it hurts. When you move against me like that...."

"Oh, Max, I'm sorry." Her whisper was distressed.

"No, no, babe. Don't be sorry. I love the way you feel next to me." He was leaving kisses all around her ear, at her temple, across to her eyes. "I just want to be able to do something about it."

Her leaden lids lifted. Even though she knew he was right, her eyes dimmed with disappointment. This was not the time for heavy kisses. She was supposed to be the practical one, wasn't she? But she wasn't acting in a practical way at all. What was it about this man that swept away her good common sense?

"Wait until tonight, beautiful. Tonight...it will be wonderful. I'm going to make slow easy love to you. Kiss every soft inch of your gorgeous body. We have the whole day tomorrow free to learn how to love each other." The hoarse hungry words were punctuated by another string of kisses, trailing from her flushed cheeks, down her throat and back up, along the column of her neck to her mouth. His hands moved too, restlessly outlining the shape of her hips, the indentation of her waist, the smooth curve of her shoulders. "God! If I don't stop neither of us will make it to work," he groaned against her lips.

Gripping her shoulders, he held her in place while he backed away a step. His breathing was harsh and unsteady. "Ah-h-h, Samantha, you are the sweetest temptation."

Like an unwelcome refrain words surfaced, repeated themselves in her brain. *Slow down. Take it easy. This is the illusion of falling in love,* she reminded herself. *You don't know him well enough to be sure.* She struggled to find her voice and put at least a part of a smile on her face. "And you're a bite of the forbidden apple yourself, Max."

He frowned at that. "Forbidden? What do you mean?"

One hand waved nervously at him. "I...we...." Her brain simply wasn't functioning efficiently enough to put any thoughts together coherently.

Suddenly the expression in his eyes softened. He folded her in his arms and drew her to him with exquisite tenderness. "Are you still worried that we don't know each other very well, darlin'? That we've progressed too quickly to Stage Two?" His chin moved against her hair as he spoke.

"Sort of," she mumbled into his chest. "Our Stage One didn't last very long."

His long fingers cradled her throat to lift her face. "'Stage One cannot be gauged in time. It can pass in months, weeks, even in hours,'" he quoted, and smiled lovingly at her stunned expression.

Samantha blinked. "You read my book," she whispered almost accusingly.

"Wasn't that the reason you gave it to me?"

"How far did you get?" she asked, almost afraid to hear the answer.

He pretended to ponder, but the masculine dimple in his cheek gave him away. "'Stage Two is marked by real and frequent sexual intimacy.'"

Samantha groaned and hid her face in his shirt. She hadn't expected him to read so far so quickly; and she certainly hadn't expected him to turn her own words around on her! She tried to think of a comeback. "'Every woman who thinks she is in love doesn't have to jump into the closest bed.'"

Unfortunately for Samantha, Max recognized the quote and finished it for her. "'But today's couples recognize that sexual compatibility is a crucial part of their romantic expectations, and they usually don't progress into Stage Two without crossing this most important threshold,'" he said very gently.

"Max!" she wailed.

He chuckled, a warm lovely vibration from deep within his chest. "Don't worry, darlin'. I'll give you time—as much as you can stand. If we don't make love tonight, we will tomorrow night, or the next day, or the next." There was a light in his eyes that belied his teasing. "And if we don't go crazy from the frustration, the anticipation might be exciting."

Samantha shook her head and glared up at him in mock exasperation. "I never should have given you that book. I have a feeling you're going to be one step in front of me all the way."

"But I'll be looking over my shoulder to make sure you're following, love." His voice was such a wonderful sound, rich and deep and movingly emotional when he spoke to her.

Samantha knew that the blissful high at the beginning of Stage Two fed on itself to grow and enlarge like a balloon. But her pleasure, her happiness, was more intense than it had ever been before. And she had never reached the point of venturing to trust a man so soon.

She had been through the stages of love, or thought she had, several times. Once, with Gregory, she had even speculated on the possibility of Stage Four. No skyrockets went off when he kissed her, but that suited her down-to-earth nature just fine. Gregory was also a psychologist and she'd assumed they had a great deal in common. Until he proposed during Stage Three, and his attitude toward marriage had been made clear. In spite of his conservative middle-class background, Gregory's concept of a relationship was one of total freedom. He considered fidelity passé. Samantha had been hurt by the revelation far more than she would admit to Gregory.

When she had finally told him a year ago that it was over between them, he hadn't seemed surprised. "You still live with a rather Victorian aspect of morality, my dear, despite your book."

Samantha had drawn herself up to her full height. "I think you misunderstand the idea behind my writings, Gregory. My intention is to prepare people for a lifetime together, to help marriage survive as an institution, not sabotage it."

"We only differ in degree. You believe in the inevitability of sex before marriage." He'd spoken carelessly. "I believe in the inevitability of sex, period."

Samantha was incensed. "Certainly not! Sex before marriage is not a prerequisite, but since it is a widespread fact in our society, couples should learn to deal with it sensibly."

Now she needed to make some sensible decisions concerning her relationship with Max. What were his feelings about fidelity? It was too soon to come right out and ask. But the way he made her feel was so far from the reasonable practical woman who had argued with Gregory, she might be another person entirely. She feared that she might wake up at some point in their relationship to find that everything had gone wrong if she didn't force herself to follow the guidelines she'd set up in her book. Maybe she should read it again, too. This feeling between the two of them was something quite marvelous; it should be nurtured and carefully encouraged so that it didn't lead to a heartbreaking confrontation.

"You seem to be thinking very serious thoughts," Max observed with a smile.

"Just...." She suddenly wrapped her arms around his waist tightly. "Oh, Max! All at once I'm afraid." That strange claustrophobic feeling returned, and instead of clinging to him she was pushing him away.

But his arms closed more tightly around her, his hands stroked her back. He seemed to sense the war going on inside her. "Don't worry, darlin'. We'll be fine."

THE BAR off the lobby at Sea Tangle was filled to overflowing by four-thirty. Word had spread quickly

She turned quickly, the movement spreading her auburn hair in a fan out from her shoulders. "Good afternoon, Mr. Townsend." The remnants of her happy smile spilled over onto the couple who stood there.

Mr. Townsend seemed taken aback for a moment by the glowing girl, but then he regained his aplomb. "My dear, this is Samantha Hyatt. Samantha, my wife, Anna."

Samantha held out her hand. "I'm so happy to meet you, Mrs. Townsend. I understand I owe my job to an idea of yours."

"And an indulgent husband, Miss Hyatt. How do you do." Anna Townsend accepted the hand as she smiled up at her husband. She hadn't missed his reaction, but she couldn't really blame the poor dear. The woman before them was stunning, with a glow that went beyond mere beauty. The sparkling expectation in her eyes, the radiance of her skin, the shimmering smile—all declared a woman in love. Still, Anna's smile was guarded when she returned her full attention to Samantha. The glowing woman had been looking at Max when they entered. Could they be...? Oh, dear.

The older man gave a rueful grin to the understanding woman beside him. Then his voice took on a softer note. "And this is our granddaughter, Janie."

The Townsends' pride in each other was obvious in their expressions, but they shared a sadness at the mention of the name. When Samantha turned to the child she knew why.

Janie was a beautiful little girl of about seven. Her dark hair was neatly braided and tied with bright red ribbons to match her dress, but there was a

that the new pianist was as beautiful as she w
ented.

Max's back was turned when Samantha pause on the threshold but, as though he felt her presence in the crowded room, he turned slowly. He leaned forward, spreading his arms wide to flatten his palms on the shining mahogany bar. The smile on his face had grown appreciatively wider by the time he'd finished his thorough visual inventory.

Back in her apartment, which had seemed so empty when he left, she had gone through her closet with a critical eye, discarding several outfits. She had bathed in scented water, shampooed her hair and dressed carefully, following her urge to be as beautiful for him as possible.

Though it was not an irrevocable decision, she told herself, she wanted to test the physical aspect of their relationship as much as he very obviously did, and she thought she wanted to do it tonight.

The expression in his eyes, bright with satisfaction, was everything she could have desired.

She wore silk the color of old gold, which reflected the golden flecks in her eyes. The braid of chains she'd worn that first day adorned her neck. A camisole, loose-fitting jacket and slim pants defined her body with elegance and subtle sensuality.

Their gazes met and clung and the crowd disappeared. They were caught together in a soundless bubble. She wondered how long they would have stood there grinning at each other like silly fools if Mr. Townsend hadn't brought them back to the present.

"Good afternoon, Samantha." The greeting came from behind her.

pinched expression on her face. Tension marred her features and her brown eyes were nervous. Her gaze darted, never settling in one place for more than a fleeting moment.

Samantha went down to her knees in instant sympathy to the child. "Hello, Janie," she said softly. "What a beautiful dress you have on. Red is my favorite color."

The compliment earned her a swift glance but no answer, no smile. However, the pleasant smile on her own face never faltered as she stood. "I should be getting to work now. Can you stay?" she asked the older woman.

Mr. Townsend answered instead. "Yes. Anna must hear you play." He took Janie's small hand in his. "Janie and I will wander around in the lobby. We can hear the music from out here. Janie loves music, don't you, sweetheart?"

The child didn't answer, as Samantha had instinctively known she wouldn't, but the nervous eyes settled for longer than usual on the piano across the room. Her heart ached for the child. *It must be a trauma of some kind,* she diagnosed with barely a thought. Suddenly she had an idea. "One afternoon I'll come in early, Janie, and give you a special concert. I have a book of the funniest songs. I used to play them all the time when I was your age. Maybe you could learn to play one."

The child still didn't speak.

"That would be lovely, wouldn't it, Janie?" said her grandfather. "Perhaps next week." He blinked the suspicious moisture from his eyes. "Thank you, Samantha." He moved off, talking to the child cheerfully.

"That was a kind offer, Miss Hyatt," Anna Townsend said quietly so as not to be overheard. Her smile was still reserved, withholding judgment. "But I'm not sure.... As you probably noticed, Janie—"

Samantha interrupted gently. "Please, call me Sam, Mrs. Townsend. Janie is a lovely child."

"And I'm Anna." Anna's gaze warmed slightly.

"It wasn't a meaningless offer, Anna," Samantha answered sincerely. Despite Anna's attitude of reserve, she already liked this woman, who displayed so much feeling in her face. "Music is sometimes a wonderful line of communication."

Anna sighed with all the pain of whatever had happened. "We've tried everything else. Why not music? Janie's problems are ...oh, you don't want to hear this."

"I understand," she said gently. Samantha knew that her years of training had given her the demeanor that invited confidences. It was occasionally very uncomfortable. Friends who poured out their stories to Samantha often regretted their revelations later and resented her for having been the one they confided in. After a few ruined friendships, Samantha had resolved never to let herself get embroiled in personal problems that clearly called for professional help. But if she could help little Janie, and if the child's grandparents wished it, she would take the chance this time.

"I'd like for us to get acquainted. I enjoy knowing the people who work for my husband," Anna told her, changing the subject. "Will you join me for a drink during your first break? I won't be able to stay after that. Janie gets restless pretty quickly."

"I'd love to," Samantha fibbed. What she would really love to do during the break was to escape to the office with Max and ravish him. She contemplated the mental picture gleefully.

Another classic symptom of Stage Two: indifference to others. She broke off the idea. Those dreams could wait. As he'd said, they had all weekend. The thought brought that radiant smile to her lips again. "I'll see you then."

Samantha was greeted with a polite round of applause as she made her way through the tables to the piano. Max was there waiting for her with a glass of sparkling water and the brandy snifter.

"You look fantastic, Sam," he murmured.

"Thanks." She glanced up with her heart in her eyes.

"And I'm going to have a hell of a time getting the right ingredients in the right glasses," he added in a lower voice.

"If I put the words to 'Feelings' with the music of 'Yankee Doodle Dandy,' it will be your fault," she countered.

His eyes lit with a tantalizing flame that warmed her, but his grin was reluctant. "It's going to be a long afternoon and evening, darlin'." He left to return to his place behind the bar.

Her gaze followed his progress for a silent moment. Then her attention was caught by a knowing teasing smile on the face of Jenny Worley. She returned it with a rueful grin and pulled the microphone arm toward her mouth. "Good afternoon, ladies and gentlemen. My name is Samantha Hyatt. I'll be happy to honor any of your requests," she said, and paused. "For songs," she added. The audience chuckled. "The only thing I won't play is 'Stella by Starlight.' I'm not *that* old."

"I'LL BET I KNOW what you need, lady," the husky voice murmured from out of the darkness behind her. She could almost see the suggestive leer on the man's face, though the figure reflected in the wall of plate glass was only a blur.

Samantha had finished playing for the night. She stood in the darkened lounge looking out of the gigantic window to the ocean beyond, waiting for Max to total the evening's receipts and deliver the money to the manager's office off the lobby.

"Do you?" she asked coolly without turning. "What do you suggest? Dinner?"

He laughed and the low masculine sound was dangerously near the curtain of her hair. "Maybe that, too," he breathed.

A delicious shiver traveled from the small of her back up her spine to the nape of her neck, where it spread over her shoulders and down her arms to her fingertips. The shiver wasn't the result of panic, but of glad relief as Max pulled her unprotesting body back against his length. Her hands rested on his forearms, which wrapped her from behind like a warm bar under her breasts. It had been a long, long time since she'd felt his strong arms around her. Surely this afternoon had happened last month, last year.

"What else do you think I need?" she whispered, letting her head fall sideways and back to nestle in the hollow of his throat.

"You need to relax in a long hot bath." The slow leisurely kiss on the side of her neck came between "long" and "hot" and increased her breathing rate sharply.

"And then you need a soothing revitalizing massage."

That left her with no breath at all, but she laughingly replied over the dryness in her throat. "I suppose I shall have to visit the hotel's spa before I go home."

"I've got a better idea. Let's have dinner downstairs and dance for a while. Then I'll take you to my place for the... um... other."

Samantha smiled and turned in his arms, only to be confronted with a Max she'd never seen before.

He was dressed in a midnight-black tuxedo, beautifully tailored in a soft worsted fabric, and a white pleated shirt of fine linen. The ends of a black bow tie dangled from beneath his loosened collar. He smiled with the endearing helpless appeal of a much younger man, tilting the full mustache. "I never could tie one of these things. Can you help me out?"

She swallowed. If she'd thought him handsome in jeans, he was devastating in dinner clothes. "Where...? When did you...?" Her hands fluttered distractedly.

Taking her hands in his, he guided them to the throat of his shirt. Automatically she began to work on the black grosgrain. "I must have been standing here for a long time." The sunstreaked color of his hair was darker than usual. She stopped what she was doing and touched it. Just as she had thought. It was wet. "You've had a shower," she said accusingly. Her fingers stroked his cheek and she sniffed. He smelled of some delicious male scent, woodsy and pleasant. "You shaved, too."

He touched her nose playfully with a fingertip. "On the button, Sherlock. I couldn't take my girl dancing dressed in jeans, now, could I?" Linking his hands behind her back, he tugged her hips closer to his and growled suggestively. "Hurry up with that tie," he ordered.

Her fingers went back to their task. "Where do you live, Max?" she asked suspiciously.

"Here," he answered innocently.

"In the hotel?" He nodded as she gave the tie a final pat. She was surprised. Living at Sea Tangle must be awfully expensive. Unless there was some sort of dormitory arrangement for employees.

He stopped the other questions that rose to her lips with a quick kiss. "I'll tell you everything you want to know over dinner, okay?" He held out his arm formally. "Shall we go?"

"Okay," she agreed, placing her hand in the crook of his elbow, but she was subdued as they walked through the lobby. A thousand questions chased themselves inside her head. The reactions of people they passed went unnoticed. The stunning couple in formal clothes, he so tall and virile, and she, dainty and shining like a golden moonbeam, were totally engrossed in each other.

Max had made reservations for them downstairs in the Dinner Club. Samantha had not been there before. As she followed the maître d' to a curved black-leather banquette she looked around with pleasure. The lighting was dim, supplemented by a profusion of candles, and on each table were fresh flowers in tiny silver containers. Pure white napery, shining flatwear and sparkling crystal set the tone for the rest of the tasteful decor. She noted the bandstand, now empty except for a selection of temporarily abandoned instruments.

The man pulled the table aside for them to slide in. When they were seated she realized that they were in a small oasis of privacy. The padded back reached above Max's head, and the only other table between them and the view of the ocean was unoccupied.

"What a lovely place!" she exclaimed. "Whoever did the decorating is a genius."

"Anna decorated everything in this hotel, down to the elevators." Max grinned. "How lucky for Abe that she has good taste, because he simply can't say no when she gets an idea. I saw the two of you talking this afternoon. Do you like her?"

"Oh, yes. She's very nice, and very sad, I think."

"I felt sure you'd notice. Little Janie hasn't spoken in two years."

"Not at all?" Samantha was shocked. The trauma was worse than she'd suspected.

Max shook his head. When he spoke again there was a guarded tension in his voice, a tightening around his eyes. "Her parents were killed in an automobile accident. She was thrown clear but they were still inside when it rolled over and caught fire. She was sitting where she had fallen, watching it burn, when they found her. She's never even cried."

"Oh, Max! How awful for her!"

"And for Abe and Anna. Janie's father was their only son." The story left a look of tragic sadness in his eyes that Samantha had wondered about. "He was my closest friend." He seemed to be about to add something when the waiter interrupted, asking if they would like a cocktail.

Max ordered champagne instead. "This is a party," he said, determinedly changing the mood. "No more somber subjects tonight."

"Champagne twice in one day?" Samantha asked, meeting his attempt at lightness, but also trying to banish the questions from her mind. "You'll spoil me!"

His smile was tender. "I wish I could spoil you, darlin'. I'd like to give you the moon. If you wanted it, that is."

Samantha felt suddenly guilty. Max couldn't afford this. The Dinner Club must be very expensive. "Nonsense. I'm not the kind of person who needs to be pampered," she told him firmly.

His eyes narrowed as he seemed to ponder. "I agree. Unless I'm very mistaken you have a practical streak that's a yard wide. You're the realist and I'm the romantic in this relationship."

Samantha wasn't sure she liked the designation of realist, but she had to admit that she was as logical as he thought her. "Why does that make me sad, Max?"

"Darlin'! I didn't mean to criticize you. Every good relationship needs a balance." He picked up her hand from where it rested on the table and held it warmly between his palms. "Our balance is perfect. Why, even our jobs mesh," he added with a grin that held a strange gleam.

At her quizzical smile he went on. "I'm a bartender and you're a piano player."

She was startled. She really didn't think of herself as a piano player, but a psychologist who, for the present, happened to be playing the piano. "I guess you're right," she said dubiously.

"Of course I am. Now if you were a psychologist

who just happened to come into the bar, I'd be beneath your notice, wouldn't I?"

"No!" Samantha denied that immediately. "No, Max. I know I acted like a snob that first day, but I don't think that way anymore."

He looked unconvinced and she twined her fingers through his to give his hand a shake. "I really don't," she whispered. Without a thought for their surroundings she leaned closer to touch her lips to his.

The action surprised him, but his eyes took fire, even as he took over the kiss. His mouth opened, then moved over her soft lips. "Ah-h-h, darlin'," he murmured into her mouth. "We weren't going to talk about serious things, were we?"

"No, we weren't," she agreed through the sensual haze his kiss created.

The band had returned to strike up an easy-listening ballad, but Max didn't ask her to dance. "I'd rather sit here close to you, by ourselves for now. We can dance later." He sat back, keeping a firm hold on her hand as he answered the question she hadn't even asked.

"I wish you'd quit doing that," she scolded with a smile that was definitely beginning to blur around the edges.

"Doing what?" He lifted her hand to his lips. His eyes kept a tenacious hold on hers as he opened her fingers. His mouth began a warm foray over her palm.

"Answering my questions before I ask them," she murmured huskily.

"Sorry." He dismissed her complaint with a grin from behind her hand. His tongue darted out and she felt the resulting shock in the depth of her stomach. "You have the sexiest voice I've ever heard. Abe called it a whiskey voice, didn't he?" He used his mustache on her palm like a sensual weapon, while his other hand dropped casually under the table to stroke her leg. "I've never heard that term before but it's descriptive. Raw, neat, like fine whiskey, and burning all the way down."

She struggled for composure. His long fingers curved around her inner thigh, using the sensual feel of the silk to heighten the effect of his touch. The stroking hand moved dangerously close to the very center of her desire. "Max, I'm already hoarse from singing," she choked. "And if you don't...."

The champagne arrived just in time to save her from embarrassing herself. She wasn't sure what she would have done—thrown him down on the seat and started tearing his clothes off, perhaps! What on earth was happening to her? During her breaks this afternoon she had speculated on the possibility of ravishing him in the office behind the bar. And now the aggressive urge, which was so uncharacteristic, was even stronger. This situation must be brought under control.

"Max, we really have to talk."

He gave a heavy sigh and reached for his glass. "I know," he said. "But first.... To us, Sam darlin'." He lifted the glass and sipped. She did the same.

"To us," she repeated firmly. "And to getting better acquainted."

His smile was rueful, and he removed his hand from her leg. "That has an ominous sound, darlin'. Do you mean that I put on this damn tux to impress you and it was all for nothing? You're not going to be seducible?"

"Seducible? Is there such a word?"

He pretended to think it over. "There is now," he finally decreed with an unrepentant grin. "I think it's very descriptive."

Samantha didn't honor the statement with an answer.

THE SHRIMP DE JONG, prepared with large Florida prawns and delicately spiced, was superb; the aspic salad, cool and tart on the tongue. Samantha declined dessert but accepted coffee, and Max had a brandy with his.

She sighed, replete. "I love living on the coast. Fresh seafood used to be such a treat that I almost feel sinful having it whenever I want."

"I know what you mean. When I was in college in Kentucky I felt the same way, so I worked on the shrimp boats in the summers just so I could have all I could eat."

He didn't notice Samantha's sudden stillness. "I don't think I could ever live very far from Florida permanently," he finished, swirling the amber liquid in the balloon glass before lifting it to sip.

College? Samantha let her head fall back against the cushion and laughed softly at herself. "Well, so much for a learning disability," she said.

"What?" She had his attention now.

She turned her head to meet his lifted brow with a self-deprecating smile. "I was trying to understand why a man with your obvious intelligence would be tending bar. I decided you must have had a learning disability." At the sound of his choked laughter her own smile faded and she went on earnestly. "A lot of very smart people have them, you know. Look at Einstein."

"Yes, darlin'," he said, trying to stifle a grin. "I know." He covered her hand where it rested on the seat between them with his big warm fingers. "Let's dance."

"But, Max. . . ." She was finally getting some information about him and she didn't want to interrupt it to dance.

"Samantha, I know I said we'd talk and I also know I'm asking a lot. But I would like to spend this evening with you on trust. I just want to be with you, to hold you, to look at you and kiss you, without a lot of weighty explanations to get through. We have plenty of time for those later. May I have tonight?"

Her eyes were a deep gold as she looked up at him. Trust. A tentative venture onto the thin ice of trust. The step was an integral and essential part of Stage Two. She suddenly realized that she was ready to take that step toward him. "Yes," she said softly.

He dipped his head to touch her lips in a sweet kiss of tender thanks. "Let's dance," he repeated in a whisper.

They moved slowly in rhythm to the love ballads for two dances, before the band switched to something livelier. When their eyes met in question their smiles grew. Tonight they were in the mood for anything, everything.

Max was quite good, thought Samantha, as her hips and shoulders wiggled in response to the beat. His tuxedo jacket was open to give him room to move, revealing the muscular tension in his wide chest and flat stomach.

When the fast number was over, the band once again switched to a ballad. Without a word Samantha went gratefully back into his arms. Her forehead reached only to his chin, and the slight dampness there from his exertion was cool. She closed her eyes blissfully, letting him guide her, lead her wherever he wanted them to go.

A thought brought forth a smile and a chuckle. "Do you want to hear a confession?" she asked huskily.

"That depends," Max answered, never breaking the smooth rhythmic flow of his steps.

"I was going to order some books. I thought that if you *did* have a learning problem I could help you with some tutoring."

His arm tightened as he took them through a tight circular spin. When it was complete he looked down at her with a rueful grin. "You want to hear a confession?"

"That depends," she mocked with a sassy quirk of her lips.

"I'm afraid I'm inclined to go along with your competition."

Her brows wrinkled perplexedly. "I don't understand."

"I've decided that I believe in the 'love zap' theory."

"Max...." Her voice was a thin shaky thread of sound.

"I love you, Samantha." He said the words, but even if he hadn't spoken she would have read the message in his eyes. "I think I've loved you from the moment I looked across the room and saw you playing the piano." Never had she seen such commitment, such tender emotion, in anyone's face.

It wasn't, of course. It wasn't love. But if she

hadn't known better, hadn't known that love has to build slowly, through stages, she might have accepted it. She might even imagine herself with the same emotion.

"But, Max...."

He stopped her with a finger over her lips. "Sh-sh. We'll debate the merits of theory later. Now I have to figure a way to convince you to let me make love to you tonight. I want so much to make you a part of me, and not just physically, that I hurt with the wanting."

She looked up into the face that was becoming so dear to her and read the sincerity there, the need, and an unfamiliar trace of uncertainty. An avowal of love was a form of trust, too. Trust that the person to whom it was made would hold it carefully. Her eyes were as soft with feeling as her voice. "You're right. We can debate later. I'd like for you to take me home and make love to me."

Max spun her in a circle, his arm tight across her back. "Your place or mine?" he murmured into her ear.

She hesitated. "Do you actually live in the hotel?"

He nodded and the dimple scored his cheek, but he didn't really smile.

"Wouldn't you like to get away for a night?" she teased.

"Your place?" He seemed pleased and she was glad she'd offered.

She nodded and smiled up at him.

"Good. I have a reason for wanting to go there." The self-confidence that was so much a part of him seemed to reassert itself as he led her off the dance floor.

6

MAX STAYED her hand when she reached automatically to turn on the lamp beside the door. "We don't need a light," he said quietly.

Samantha looked around the bright room and agreed. Moonlight flooded through the glass doors and across the carpet, making artificial illumination both unnecessary and unwelcome. She moved forward to stand waiting while he fixed the chain and checked the lock.

Her relaxed posture didn't give any hints of her inner trepidation. Fear had no part in it. All the way home she'd thought about the night ahead, and she was quite simply anxious about possibly being a disappointment to him. Her sexual encounters with Gregory had been intermittent, and if she'd had to describe them, adequate would have been the word she'd use. But she wanted this to be more than adequate. Much more.

Max came to her. Silently, with a weightless touch at the small of her back, he steered her to the large dark silhouette that was the grand piano.

She looked up, a question in her eyes. He sat down and slid across the bench, making room for her. When she didn't sit he reached for her hand to pull her down beside him. He lifted her fingers to his lips in a gesture that touched her with its old-world courtliness. "Now," he said in a voice as soft as the moonlight. "Play a love song for me."

She laughed huskily and rubbed her cheek against the sleeve of his jacket with a kittenish movement. "Max, you've been listening to me play all afternoon and evening," she argued gently. "Most of those were love songs."

"But not just for me." He pushed aside the collar of her jacket and laid a tender kiss on the curve of her shoulder. "I want one all my own." A whisper of silk and the jacket was gone. His hand went to the braid of gold chains where it rested on her neck. He traced it down between her breasts to its lowest point and hooked a finger there.

The finger was on a level with her stomach, and she inhaled an unsteady breath.

"That first day when you came to apply for the job, you were wearing this necklace." His murmur dropped to a low, almost mesmerizing whisper.

She nodded, swallowing with difficulty.

"You had on a sweater that clung to your beautiful curves like the wind to a sail. The chain had caught around your breast. Like this." He spread the chain over the outer curve, careful not to touch her. "I could hardly take my eyes off it. I have a fantasy, darlin', that you'll play a love song just for me and afterward I'll make love to you wearing nothing but this chain." His head dipped forward under her chin and she felt his lips on the pulse at her throat.

She was unable to keep her own head erect under the weight of seduction and desire in his speech. It fell back, exposing her to the warmth of his mouth. Her right hand came up to comb through his thick silky hair. She didn't want to play the piano right now, she thought fretfully. Music was the last thing she wanted to think about.

"Please," he murmured, and she sighed. How could you argue with a man like him? He lifted his head to catch her gaze in the depths of his eyes and smiled at her unspoken assent. "Thank you, darlin'."

Caught unequivocably in the eternal spell of his eyes, she raised her left hand, stretching her fingers in search of a chord. The harmony circled their heads, lingered in the air for a moment and dissipated, leaving an echoing vibration.

Again her fingers slid over the smooth ivory and ebony keys, casting around, seeking; but this time they exerted no pressure, as though the choice of music were locked inside the piano and needed just the perfect touch for release.

The moonlight turned everything to shades of black and white and all the variations of gray in between. It silvered one side of Max's strong face as he looked down at her, leaving the other side in dark shadow and reminding her of a beautiful painting she'd once seen.

He shifted slightly, giving her space without withdrawing the warmth of his body. His long arm crossed diagonally behind her back, not touching, to take the weight of his torso on that hand.

And then the combination of tone and melody merged to flow forth by its own choice, as the Prelude in F, written by Chopin to the woman he loved, George Sand, found its release in her fingers. The notes were true under her touch, and sensitively poignant.

Max recognized the piece. He smiled and placed a kiss of appreciation on her bare shoulder.

The music, played sostenuto—lovingly, feeling—was a measured declaration of her emotion. The thread of its harmony seemed to link them in this moment out of time with the lovers of over a century ago.

And when the piece was finished, when the notes faded from the present, from this moment, in this room, Samantha knew that the melody would forever remain impressed on her heart as a part of the memory of this remarkable evening.

Without speaking, Max stood. He leaned down to lift her, one arm under her knees, one behind her shoulders. The long auburn hair spilled over his arm.

Linking her hands behind his neck, Samantha nestled her face into the hollow of his throat. Her lips found the pulse that throbbed there.

His arms were firm and sure and his footsteps unhurried as he made his way to the bedroom. Neither of them spoke, though even in the muted light their eyes said volumes. The lingering spell of the music and their awareness of each other overshadowed the need for words, at least for now.

When he reached the bed he released her legs, letting her toes touch the floor. Her arms were still linked behind his neck. She used them to pull his head down until their lips were only a breath apart. His lips brushed teasingly over hers, once, twice, three times, until with a soft moan she stretched herself to the limit of her height and reached for a deeper kiss.

As though the sound from her throat was a signal,

his arms tightened and his mouth submerged hers in a swirling tumble of erotic response. His tongue thrust inside her lips in hungry demand, and she answered joyfully, accepting the intimate challenge.

Finally he broke off, his breathing harsh and irregular, to move an inch or two away. He held himself firmly in check but his fingers were unsteady as they searched for the small golden buttons at the front of the camisole. It seemed to take an eternity for him to free them, so Samantha used the time to tug at the bow tie she had tied so neatly a few hours ago.

The onyx studs on his shirt gave her some trouble. The tip of her tongue touched the corner of her mouth in concentration. When she finally finished, she was as breathless as he. Holding them in one hand, looking at the vertical band of tanned, hair-roughened skin between the sides of his shirt, she swallowed heavily.

His deep chuckle brought her eyes up and increased her apprehension. "Why are you laughing at me?" she complained in a whisper. Suddenly she realized that her camisole was parted, too. Just slightly, nothing revealed, but she felt shy. The gold chain hung free between her breasts.

Max framed her face with hands that were infinitely tender and smiled lovingly at her. "Because you are so solemn, my love. You look like you're about to be tested for another doctorate."

"I...I'm...I guess I feel solemn. Maybe you'll be disappointed." Her tawny eyes darkened to a toasty velvety amber.

He took the studs from her hand and tossed them on the table next to the bed. "You're the doctor, darlin'. Don't you know that we all have those doubts?"

"Not you." It was a statement, not a question. Max, whose self-confidence was unwavering, couldn't be unsure of himself. Even the glimpse of uncertainty he'd shown at the Dinner Club had been so fleeting she wasn't sure she hadn't imagined it.

He dipped his head to touch his lips to her cheek, her eyes. "Yes, me. I feel like a kid with his first woman. What if I don't please you?" His voice was huskily imperfect, slightly faltering. "What if I hurt you?"

"You won't...." She wanted to reassure him.

"You're so tiny and I'm—" He broke off, taking her hand and guiding it to his hard arousal.

Samantha was shocked at his action and at the size of the throbbing maleness under her fingers.

"I'm terrified I'll go too fast. Or frighten you." He folded her into a tight embrace and buried his face in her hair. "God, Samantha," he moaned in an emotional rasp. "I love you so much. Do you think I'm not afraid that it won't be perfect for you?"

Her heart melted at his words. Suddenly all her doubts vanished like wispy summer clouds before an ocean breeze. Her arms wrapped around his back, pressing him to her. "Max, my darling, it may not be perfect...."

He raised his head to look down at her, chagrin in his eyes. "Don't be so damned practical. Not now," he ordered hoarsely.

She went on as though he hadn't interrupted. "But if it isn't, we'll just have to keep trying until we get it right."

Heavy lashes shielded the sapphire gaze from her for a brief moment. When they lifted, his eyes blazed with relief and a hunger that she'd never seen before.

The camisole fell to the floor along with the tiny scrap that was a strapless bra. Then he tenderly looped the chain around the curve of one upthrust breast. "*That* is sexy," he rasped. His hands were trembling noticeably when they reached for the hook fastener of her slacks. At last she stood before him clad only in bikini panties and the chain. His eyes traveled in wonder over her. He took in a deep shuddering breath and whispered with a yearning that was awesome in its intensity, "You are the most beautiful...." He seemed totally absorbed by the picture she made, unable to finish the sentence.

Samantha felt no self-consciousness now, only a quiet pride that he was pleased with her. She stepped forward to push the shirt off his broad shoulders. Her fingers roamed over his chest, the abrasion of the wiry hair adding its tactile embellishment to her already spinning senses. "And you are everything a man should be," she breathed almost soundlessly. Her nails drew slow circles around his flat male nipples, bringing forth a sharp gasp.

"Dear heaven!" His control was brittle now. It would take very little to crack it wide open.

Her hands provided the extra push as they drifted down, following the direction of the vee of hair that pointed into the waistband of the tuxedo slacks. Before she could open them, Max swung her up into his arms.

His knee depressed the edge of the mattress. She could read his barely controlled desire in the pulsing of a muscle in his throat, in the darkening of his blue eyes to a mysterious midnight color. He laid her on the bed, placing her head on the pillow, and tugged the panties free of her hips and legs. Then he staightened, never taking his eyes from hers, to rid himself of slacks, underpants, socks and shoes, almost in one motion.

Samantha caught her breath at the sight of the magnificent man who stood before her. Broad shoulders, lean narrow hips, thighs that were muscular and hard, all testified to a superb example of masculinity.

He returned instantly to sit on the edge of the bed, hip to hip, facing her. The gold chain winked at him in the moonlight.

Slowly, with a return on control, he gently put a warm hand on her bare stomach, as though it was something he'd waited all his life to do. It was a symbolic gesture reflected in the masterful expression that chiseled his features, a gesture of undisputed possession.

Samantha recognized it as such, and thought fleetingly and in bewilderment that she really should be taking exception to his assumption of proprietary rights. But not now. Not now when her blood was racing through her body to nourish all the secret places, readying them for a glorious experience. Not now when her pulse throbbed with passion, with need, with desire for this wonderful virile man. She twisted under his hand and a soft cry escaped from her throat. "Max, please."

At last his other hand, which had been resting casually on his knee, came up to join its mate, and they cupped her breasts. Her sigh was one of rich satisfaction.

Tenderly and skillfully, with an indolent circular massage, his palms brought the budding nipples to full bloom. He leaned forward until his warm breath caressed her as erotically as his talented fingers, stroking and squeezing gently. "I've dreamed of this since the first moment I saw that damned gold rope twining under what I wanted to touch," he whispered hoarsely. "I've dreamed of your beautiful breasts in my hands, under my lips—" his kiss brushed one throbbing tip "—in my mouth."

And suddenly the rhythm of his caress became demanding. His tongue flicked the hardened nipple. She felt the pulling sensation deep between her thighs as he engulfed her completely with his moist hungry mouth.

Her hands twisted into his hair, discovering the shape of his skull, drawing him even closer as her excitement began to build, sending her heart on a reckless untamed spree in her chest.

He shifted and she felt the weight, the long-wished-for weight of his body, crushing her onto the mattress, heating every inch of her with his barely controlled passion. His hands left their treasures to seek another more intimate spot, wending their way over her waist, down her stomach to the soft triangle at the joining of her thighs. He found her damp and warm and waiting, and caught his breath.

Propping himself on his elbows he looked down into her eyes, in his a blurred dazed question.

Her smile was the smile of Eve, of Helen, of Cleopatra, soft and sensual, willing, with an eager hunger of her own. Her fingers traced a path to his stomach and around to clench the muscles of his hips, urging him to fill her.

Carefully, breathing with an effort, he probed gently, and her hips arched up to meet him as her eyes closed and she gave herself up to pure sensation. He murmured indistinctly as he sank at last into the cradle of her womanliness. For a moment he was still.

Samantha's head was thrown back, her hair in wild disarray, a strand caught in the corner of her mouth. Max tenderly smoothed it away and replaced it with his lips in a kiss of loving praise. "You take me so perfectly, my only love," he whispered weakly. And then he began to move, slowly, skillfully, bringing into play muscles that would stimulate the most pleasure for her. His thrusts became more and more powerful, more and more masterful, but always careful. In his dominion over her senses he took everything from her and gave everything in return.

Samantha gasped and clutched at his back in a desperate attempt to anchor herself to the earth, but it was not to be. He took her with him, outside the bounds of this world to another, where, without warning, stars exploded inside her head and her slender body was reduced to convulsive energy.

A moment later she felt his potent life-giving force pulse into her, his thick ragged voice calling her name, seeking deliverance from an unknown danger. Her arms tightened protectively around him in this moment of man's ultimate vulnerability.

Their dewy spent bodies relaxed together as one, their arms still clinging, lips whispering tiny endearments between kises. Their hands roamed restlessly over each other's features; eyes unbelieving, searching for reassurance that the experience had been as meaningful and beautiful for one as it had been for the other.

At last Max rolled to the side, taking her with him, imprisoning her legs with his powerful thighs, her slight body with his arms, as though he never intended to release her.

It took a while for their breathing to return to a normal rate. By then, a delicious languid feeling had invaded Samantha's limbs. She never wanted to move again. If she could remain forever in Max's arms like this she would be happy. A smile curved her lips, and he felt it.

He tucked his chin down to meet her smile with a satisfied male grin. But she wasn't fooled. She remembered his moment of frailty and loved him all the more because of it.

Her brows climbed. Love? She hadn't used the word, not even to herself. Love was a culmination of feelings and was reached after a series of steps. What was this, then? This overwhelming emotion she felt in the security of his arms?

"What are you thinking?" he asked huskily.

She ran her fingers across the mustache, smoothing the full hair. "I think I just realized why people call it love."

His eyes flared.

"It isn't really love, you know. Not the Stage Four kind," she told him gently. "But it is a potent overpowering emotion, isn't it?"

He laughed and his arms almost crushed her. "Yes, my love, it is. And if you won't put the name to it yet, I'll settle for 'potent and overpowering emotion.'"

"I know you think I'm being unreasonable, Max. But—"

He interrupted her with a soft kiss on her upturned lips. "You don't mind if *I* call it love, do you?"

She snuggled closer. "No, I don't mind," she admitted. As a matter of fact she was surprised to realize that it gave her a nice warm feeling inside, sort of like waking up as a child on Christmas morning to find that Santa Claus had brought her heart's desire. No wonder people were so willing to declare themselves in love. "I don't mind at all." The words were a sleepy murmur, spoken in rhythm to Max's caressing hand on her back, and she closed her eyes.

WHEN SAMANTHA AWOKE again, it was to an enchanting continuation of the sensual massage. But now his voice called her name urgently, his mouth and hands moved over her in gentle demand, insisting that she come back to consciousness to participate fully in another glorious adventure.

She rolled onto her back. Max knelt over her, one hair-roughened leg between her thighs, and she arched her back. The movement thrust her breasts upward to brush against his chest, eliciting a deep hungry groan from his throat. His lips and tongue were exploring the tiny shell of her ear, and the sound sent a soft blast of his warm breath across her cheek.

"Oh, Sam," he muttered thickly. "I want you again...and again...and again. God, darlin', I'll never have enough of you!" His teeth nibbled at her lobe, sending delightful chills over her. Then he began a slow tortuous trail down her body, pausing for an interminable length of time at her sensitive breasts. He used his tongue, his teeth and his lips to bring her to a mindless writhing state of delight; she was begging for more even as she begged for release. She clutched his shoulders, digging her nails into the hard muscle in greedy demand.

"Max! Oh, Max. Please!" she cried finally in desperate need.

He lifted her hips and surged forward into her, his strokes merging powerfully with her rhythm, taking over, to direct them both to a flaming fulfillment. At the moment of release her arms tightened around his neck in a gesture of possession that she wasn't even aware of, and she hung on as though her life, her very existence, depended on their unity. "Hold me, hold me," she begged.

"Yes, love. Always," he promised huskily.

ON THE COAST, night gave way quickly to day. There was no soft dawn surrendering its shadowed colors; instead, a sudden blaze of sunlight heralded the morning.

A warm saffron beam took the same liberties with Samantha's body that Max had taken only hours before. In her dreams the ray of sun became a gentle fingertip and she twisted restlessly under its heat.

"Good morning," said a husky voice against her ear.

She opened her eyes to see a broad expanse of hard male chest. Her hair was tangled beneath the arm across her shoulders and she had to give a painful little jerk to free it before she could look up into Max's face. "Good morning." She greeted him with a soft smile. "Have you been awake long?"

"Awhile," he answered absently. His free hand came up to cradle the side of her face. "You look pretty in the morning, soft and warm and fluffy."

"Fluffy?" The smile grew.

He raised his head to place a light kiss on the tip of her nose and then fell back onto the pillow. "Well, delightfully disheveled," he amended, looking at the ceiling.

There was something on his mind, she thought, surprised by the feeling of dread that wiped the smile from her face. Had she disappointed him after all? No, she couldn't believe that, not after the beautiful blending of their bodies. "I like 'fluffy,'" she informed him and nestled closer, unknowingly seeking comfort with her head tucked under his chin.

His hand began to stroke distractedly along her arm to her elbow and back again to her shoulder where it lingered with a touch that definitely wasn't loverlike. "Sam, do you think we should talk now?" He sounded very serious.

For some reason his tone disturbed her even more, and she forced herself to answer lightly. "On an empty stomach?"

He sighed. "You're right. And I couldn't keep my mind on the subject with a beautiful woman in my arms. Why don't you make us some coffee, while I make use of your shower?"

A beautiful woman? *He makes it sound like any one would do,* she thought petulantly. She had looked forward to showering together, but instead of protesting, she silently rose from the bed and went to the closet for a robe.

He didn't even seem to notice when she left the room heading for the other bath.

HE'S MARRIED. *I know it! He's married. He'll probably come in with some stupid platitude about his wife's not understanding him.*

Samantha had stewed for the entire ten minutes it took the coffee to perk. Max's distraction and moodiness upon waking had indicated that there was a major hurdle to be faced this morning. And she had convinced herself that the only complication strong enough to put that expression in his eyes would be awful. If he was married it would be the most awful thing she could imagine.

She jerked the belt of her robe tighter with an angry gesture and poured a mug of coffee for herself. Let him get his own! She leaned one hip against the Formica counter and stared out through the glass to the horizon. The bright sunshine was under attack from a few gathering clouds. "Poor woman," she said out loud.

"What?"

The voice came from the doorway behind her and she whirled, steadying the mug between her hands. "I said 'poor woman,'" she repeated trying to ignore the feelings of desire this man could arouse within her at just a glance.

He wore the trousers of the tuxedo and was sliding his arms into the pleated shirt as he walked into the kitchen. The curling hair that covered his chest was still darkened by dampness.

"Your wife!" she added so that there would be no misunderstanding as to the identity of the poor woman. She certainly didn't want him to assume she meant herself.

"My what?"

His astonishment was genuine, she would have

sworn to that. Samantha began to feel like a fool. "You're not married?" she asked in a small voice.

"Where the hell did you get an idea like that?"

She raked her lower lip with her teeth. "You looked so...thoughtful this morning....almost guilty."

He planted his hands on his hips and glared down at her for what seemed an incredibly long time. Then he shook his head slowly, as though he simply could not believe what she had said.

Samantha was in total sympathy. She couldn't believe what she'd said, either. This man unsettled her, threw her completely off base. "I'm sorry."

"Sorry? Sorry! My God, Samantha! You really *do* have a tendency to jump to conclusions about me, don't you?" He was furious and the sheer size of him made his fury intimidating. "I've told you that I love you. Do you think I'm the kind of man who would do that if I was married to someone else?"

"No." Her voice shrank further.

Grim-featured, he turned from her and combed an impatient hand through his hair. "I can see we really do have to talk. You don't have a hell of a lot of trust in this bartender, do you?"

Bartender? Was he still dwelling on that? She had completely forgotten about her original aversion to his job. Well, the subject of bartending was one thing she'd have to clear up immediately; bury it forever. She raised her chin determinedly. "That has absolutely nothing to do with it. I told you last night, I don't care what you do for a living."

He glanced over his shoulder as he reached into the cabinet for a mug. His brow lifted in a doubtful curve.

"I mean it, Max," she said earnestly in an attempt

to make up for her earlier blunder. "I haven't even thought about that for a long time."

He gave a short nod but didn't speak.

"It...it was your expression," she went on. "It made me wonder if you were regretting...if I wasn't good enough."

The mug hit the counter with a force that threatened its handle. In two strides he was beside her. He took her shoulders in his hands and sat her in the chair.

He crouched over her until their noses were almost touching. "For a beautiful woman you have quite an inferiority complex. Now, watch closely. I am going to demonstrate some facial expressions. This is serious—" he pulled a long thoughtful look "—as in 'We have to talk and it's very important to me.'"

His face twisted into a parody of a leer. "This is 'I've got the hots for you, my lovely, and you'd better watch out.'" Then his brows came together in a dark glower. "*This* is 'angry.'" He finally released her shoulders and sighed, sitting back on his haunches. "And I haven't got one for 'I'm disappointed in your sexual performance,' because it isn't relevant and never will be." He watched her carefully for a reaction.

Samantha's emotions were fighting between tears and laughter. But laughter won, barely. She catapulted herself into his arms, throwing him off-balance, and they both ended up sprawled on the floor while she hugged him and drew back and hugged him again.

She couldn't believe she was being forgiven so easily for her stupid assumption. "You wonderful,

wonderful man. You're the best lover in the world, and the most handsome, most thoughtful. I don't deserve you," she babbled extravagantly between damp kisses.

Max finally got her under control by the simple method of pinning her to the floor with his large body. He began to return her kisses, but his were much less frivolous, and when he finally raised his head he muttered huskily, "Now may I have my coffee?"

7

"WHO GOES FIRST?" Max demanded in a rough voice.

Samantha looked at him in surprise, but he was leaning into the curve of the piano, his eyes fixed on a point beyond the glass door somewhere over the ocean.

He heaved a deep sigh and shot her a glance that held both amusement and regret. "You're sure this is necessary? We could simply take each other on trust," he offered, looking down into his coffee. He swirled the liquid slightly and took a swallow. "I'm not interested in rehashing old memories as much as I am in making new ones, Samantha."

They could. They could avoid anything resembling an awkward subject for now. But what would happen later? They would eventually find themselves emotionally isolated from each other, and she could not endure isolation from him. The thought was the closest she'd come to admitting to herself that *love* might be a good word, after all. Of course that didn't change the fact that the idea of permanency was still distasteful.

The stages were becoming confused. She shouldn't be feeling this way until the latter half of Stage Three. She straightened her shoulders. "Tell me about yourself, Max," she answered with professional determination.

He had been quiet during breakfast, very quiet, giving toneless answers to the most innocuous questions. For some reason he had erected a shield of defensiveness that she didn't understand. Why should he be hesitant about their getting to know each other better?

Samantha knew instinctively that this would not be an easy time for either of them, but it had to be worked through, so she answered his unspoken question without it being asked. "Max, being emotionally honest does involve some risk, but we must be willing to open up to each other if this relationship is to go anywhere." She curled her bare feet under her on the sofa and sipped her coffee. "You already know a lot about me, so why don't you start?"

"Okay." He turned toward her and propped both elbows behind him on the top of the piano. The stance tugged at the studs he had replaced in his shirt, and emphasized his broad chest. Carelessly he hooked one ankle across the other, drawing her attention to the strength of his thighs. His eyes were their brightest blue as they fixed thoughtfully on her.

Samantha indulged in a thoroughly exciting scan of his long lean body and swallowed around a sudden dryness in her mouth. By the time he was ready to begin, she had almost forgotten what it was that they were supposed to be talking about.

Max smiled slowly, knowingly. "You do the same thing to me, darlin'."

Involuntarily her eyes dropped to check the truth of his statement, and her face turned a wild color.

Shoving his hands into the pockets of his black

trousers he frowned at her. She had an idea, however, that the frown was directed inward, toward himself. "Dr. Hyatt, I'm shocked." He tried to tease, but the words came out sounding hollow.

She hid her face in the steam rising from her coffee mug, thinking irrelevantly that it couldn't be any hotter than the blood rushing through her veins.

"I'm originally from Jacksonville," Max began. "My father is retired, and he and my mother live in Jacksonville during the winter. They have a summer home in North Carolina. I have one brother and two sisters." His voice was a monotone.

Samantha's eyes had flown to him at the first words. She had assumed he was more or less alone in the world, as she herself was. *Jumping to conclusions again,* she reminded herself ruefully.

"They don't have much to do with me." He looked away from her, his eyes drawn again to the sea. His normal healthy color had paled. "I'm a disappointment to them. They think I'm totally lacking in ambition." He paused. "I suppose I am...their kind of ambition anyway. Something happened a couple of years ago, ah, well...." He shrugged. "I'm getting ahead of my story."

She watched the muscle in his jaw as it clenched and relaxed, clenched and relaxed. The subject of his family was extremely difficult for him for some reason, and all at once a feeling of premonition, of dread, gripped her. She wished she hadn't insisted so strongly. "Max...."

"I'm the renegade in the family. Or have been for the last two years." He went on as though she hadn't interrupted, speaking to himself, not her. "Rebellion didn't come easy for me. In fact, my parents had always been so supportive that I never thought it necessary to rebel while I was young.

"I did exactly what I was expected to do for thirty-four years. And then one day I woke up to face the fact that I was a pompous ass and arrogant as hell. I'm glad you didn't know me then, Samantha. You wouldn't have liked me at all."

He paused to swipe a hand down his face. The gesture reminded her of a game she had played as a child, where you wiped a smile on and off, but Max left no smile. The expression on his face revealed a hitherto hidden mask of isolation.

The sight twisted like a knife in her heart, and all of a sudden she felt the stirrings of panic. He seemed to retire within himself, shutting her out. It was as though when she'd unlocked the door to another part of his life she had opened a Pandora's box of self-censure and unhappiness that he was retreating into.

She didn't want Max to withdraw from her, she thought frantically. What had she begun? Suddenly she wanted to stop it. She looked around the room, ridiculously seeking assistance from inanimate objects. Where was her precious theory now? She wanted to cry, *No, Max! I'll take you on trust. I'll take you any way. Just don't do this to yourself.*

Setting the mug carefully on the table in front of her, she uncurled her legs and got to her feet. "Max," she said weakly. She crossed the floor quickly on shaky legs to where he stood and took his mug from his hand. She actually had to loosen his fingers. That scared her even more.

She was a psychologist, supposed to be able to handle such situations, but she knew that she wouldn't be able to handle this, not when it concerned this man. She was too close. She shared his hurt as though it were her own. "Come and sit beside me," she urged, hoping he wouldn't notice how her own hands were trembling.

He looked at her with a blank stare as if he'd forgotten who she was. Then he shook his head to clear it. "I'm all right," he protested, bitterness clouding his eyes. "I lay awake, watching you while you slept, wondering how the hell I was going to get through this explanation without having you end up despising me. I thought about lying, but then I decided that you really should hear it all, my love, so you can judge the man you spent last night with."

His voice was cold, so cold that she shivered in response. "I'm not here to judge you, Max," she said gently. "And if this is too painful...."

Finally he let himself be led to the sofa. With a soft shove she sat him down. "Painful!" he exclaimed harshly. "Gratitude is what I should feel. Overwhelming gratitude." He leaned forward, elbows on his knees to hide his face in his big hands.

His next words were delivered in almost wondering abstraction. "The Townsends understood. That was what was so strange. They understood when my own parents didn't."

Samantha forced herself to take a calming breath. She had seen the warmth and affection the Townsends felt for Max. Anna had seemed to light up yesterday when Max joined them during the first of Samantha's breaks. And she had told Samantha that Abe thought of Max as another son. There was something very wrong here, she thought, but she forced her voice to a level of reasonable restraint.

"Then don't you think it's time you forgave yourself for this guilt you're carrying?" she asked quietly.

He dropped his hands, letting them dangle between his knees, and slowly turned his head to look at her. "How can I?"

He should let the emotion out, rather than keep it hidden behind the mask of control, the therapist in her said, but the woman in her ached to comfort him. She had to steel herself not to cry out at the suffering in his face, but she couldn't control the instinct to hold out her arms.

He came into them like a child seeking comfort at his mother's breast. His arms closed around her in a convulsive embrace, and he sank his face into the curve of her neck.

Whatever it was that he had done—and she was sure it was inadvertent—he was blaming himself far more than others blamed him. She brushed back the lock of fawn-colored hair that fell over his brow.

"I'll never be able to forgive myself," he said quietly.

"Max, let's talk about it later," she said hastily.

He wrenched himself free of her arms and settled back against the sofa cushions, refusing to meet her eyes. "Later? Time won't make it any easier. No. We've started. You may as well hear the whole story."

She put a restraining hand on his arm. "Only if you think it will help," she said very carefully.

The suggestion obviously caught him off-balance. He looked at her through lowered lashes, considering. She could tell that the thought of her as a psychologist hadn't occurred to him before that moment. Then his lips curled in a half deprecating, half thoughtful smile. "You're the doctor." He took her hand. "You know—" he told her with the first glimmer of optimism in his eyes she'd seen since breakfast "—it just might."

She returned the squeeze of his fingers.

"I'm not sure where to begin...I suppose in college. That's where I met Chip." He looked down at their clasped hands. "Chip was Abe Townsend III, Anna and Abe's son. I was Max Stanwood III. But Chip's name was chosen for him in an attempt to build tradition, and mine was given to me in propagation of tradition. Chip's grandfather came to America on a cattle boat. His family's three generations had worked like hell to get to where they were, and mine had been handed it all on a silver platter.

"We hit it off from the first. He was good fun, charming and as smart as a whip." A reminiscent smile curved his lips. "We raised a lot of hell together; had some great times. I started spending my summers here in Destin rather than in Jacksonville. Abe and Anna were like a second set of parents. I think they were as proud of my accomplishments as they were of his."

When he returned his head to the cushion, she was relieved to see that his features wore a measure of tranquility.

He explained, "Chip was at the University of Virginia on a full scholarship. Those aren't easy to get."

"Virginia? I thought you said Kentucky."

"That's where I did my undergraduate work. I went to law school in Virginia."

"You're a lawyer?" Samantha was stunned. Max didn't fit her idea of a lawyer at all. She remembered his surprise when he had found out she was a psychologist. He must have thought the same of her.

He traced the knuckles of her hand with a forefinger. "I am... was... a judge."

"A judge? At your age?" That was even more surprising.

Bitter sarcasm returned to color his voice as he continued. "Oh, yes. I was a boy wonder. Graduated magna cum laude. Returned home to take my rightful place in the firm my grandfather founded. I bought a house on the right street, won some landmark cases, became engaged to the right woman, and when the judgeship became vacant, I was the logical one to fill it, despite my age. I was thirty-three.

"Chip had joined the firm, too, but he was never happy there. It was high-powered, ulcer-producing, money-making law. He didn't stay long. He went out on his own, helping people who couldn't afford our firm's high fees. He tried to talk me into joining him, but I wasn't interested.

"We were like brothers, much closer than I ever was to my own older brother. I was best man at Chip's wedding.... Anyway, when I was appointed judge it all began to change. I guess you might say I contracted a terminal case of 'robitis.'"

She had never heard the term before. "'Robitis'?" she repeated.

He gave a harsh laugh. "'Robitis' is the feeling you get upon donning the judge's robe: you are as close to God as it's possible to be on earth. Most judges feel it, and the majority of them manage to fight it off, but not me. I was too impressed with my own importance and had no hesitancy about throwing my weight around.

"Chip and his wife began to come up with some pretty weak excuses not to see me. I guess I wasn't very good company." Suddenly he surged to his feet, dropping her hand, and began to pace, his long legs striding across the carpet.

"I did know the law. There's no doubt about that. But when it came to applying it to people, I lacked something, a sense of humanity, perhaps. My fiancée broke our engagement. It didn't hurt a bit. It had been more of a business arrangement than an engagement anyway, and there were always other women. But when Chip—my best friend—began to criticize some of my rulings, I felt like I'd been betrayed."

Max finally stopped his pacing and stood in front of the window again, hands in his pockets, staring at nothing. His voice took on the emptiness that she'd noticed before and now recognized as a self-protecting device. If you didn't let emotion show, you could fool yourself into believing that emotion wasn't there. What wasn't there couldn't hurt.

"Chip was appointed to a criminal case—a young boy charged with armed robbery—that was to be tried before me. He did everything possible to effect a change of venue, and of course I heard about it. It made me furious to think that he would question my impartiality. To make a long story short, the boy was found guilty."

Max stood very still for a long time before he finally took up the story in a voice that was so faint she had to strain to hear. "Three months later another man confessed to the crime." The silence in the room was absolute as Samantha watched Max's struggle for control.

"The evidence...the jury..." she whispered.

"It wasn't a jury trial. Two witnesses had sworn to the boy's presence at the scene of the robbery, but the boy's girlfriend and parents had also sworn that he'd been at home." He raked a hand through his hair in an impatient gesture. "The kid had been in trouble before. I chose to take the word of the witnesses, in spite of Chip's belief in the boy's innocence.

"After the real criminal confessed, Chip came to my chambers to have me sign the order for the boy's release. He was rightfully irate. After he had cussed me out, he told me in no uncertain terms that I was an arrogant jackass and a lousy judge. I really took offense at that. Errors in judgment are not that uncommon, I told him."

"That's true, Max," she interjected.

He glanced over his shoulder. "Thanks for trying to defend me, but Chip was right. I had lost all my objectivity in the pursuit of success," Max said heavily. "He told me he never wanted me to come near him or his family again. They left that afternoon, headed toward Destin, and I never saw him alive again.

"His accusation was a terrible blow to my self-esteem." A harsh raw laugh escaped him. "That was actually my first reaction—totally selfish—thinking about the effect on *me*. Then I began to really think about what I'd become, and it finally hit me. The man who had done everything right, who was invincible, had done something wrong. In law school we were all such idealists. But in the race for success you tend to forget your ideals.

"Except for Chip. He never lost sight of the fact that what it all boils down to, the bottom line, is that you have to live with yourself.

"It was only a few weeks later that Chip and his

wife were killed in the automobile accident. In a way I suppose I felt partly responsible, though I realize I'm only trying to punish myself because I'm still alive and Chip, who knew more about the real meaning of the law and was a better lawyer than I'll ever be, is dead."

MAX'S SHOULDERS SLUMPED, weighted with the memory of his friend's death. After a week of trying to lose his senses in a bottle, he'd resigned his judgeship.

His family had come on the run—his brother, both sisters—to urge him to reconsider. When their arguments had no effect, they had brought on the big guns.

His father and mother had flown down from North Carolina in the family plane. He would never forget that confrontation if he lived to be a hundred. He had always thought of his father as a just man, demanding but basically kind. Of course, his relationship with his father had never been tested. He'd never refused to do what was asked of him before, never failed to live up to his father's expectations. "These things happen. Don't let it change your course," Maxwell II had said, as though it was only a simple mistake.

From that conversation Max had realized that the judgeship and the resultant political power that went with it were far more important to the firm and to the family than the loss of one lawyer or the remorse of a son. He also realized to his horror that he would have reacted in the same way if someone else had been in his situation.

The death of his closest friend and the disillusionment he'd felt at his family's reaction had seemed like a divine compounding of punishment, a judgment against him. He left immediately to come to Destin, and he had never returned to Jacksonville. He supposed he'd had some vague intention of being a consolation to Abe and Anna, but actually it had turned out just the opposite.

Another month had been spent wandering like a lost soul on the beaches and waterfront of Destin before Max finally asked Abe for a job. He hadn't been sure of his own motives. Perhaps he wanted to offer himself as a replacement—never a substitute—body to help make up for the one that now lay in the coldness of a grave.

And in his magnanimous compassion, even in the face of his own grief, Abe had obliged. The single room at Sea Tangle had become home.

At times Max had felt that the burden of grief and guilt he had carried for two years would bury him. Slowly, with the help of Abe and Anna, the two people who understood, he had begun to pull out of the pit of wretchedness, to take an interest in the world around him, to live again. They had become his family. "I've learned to live with the guilt, in a way. But it will always be there," he said almost to himself.

As he looked out the window he noticed dark clouds settling against the horizon, blocking the sunshine in eerie prophecy of an approaching storm. The surf churned below him, surging and ebbing with the same turbulence he felt inside.

What would he see in Samantha's eyes? Disgust? Revulsion? He didn't think he could endure either. His palms began to sweat. Only a few minutes ago he had seen desire there and the thrill that shot through him had left him breathless. But then he'd stopped to wonder as he was wondering now—would he ever see desire in her eyes again now that she knew the whole truth?

This remarkable woman who was so damnably practical and so sweetly sexy, who had taught him to laugh once more, had somehow become so vital to him that he wasn't sure he could continue breathing without her. What would he do if he had destroyed that "potent overpowering emotion"? She had come into his life like a second chance. Slowly, fearfully, he turned to look at her.

She had moved with silent tread to stand beside him. When he turned she slid an arm around his waist and he automatically pulled her close. Holding his breath, he forced himself to lift his other hand, to cradle her jaw and tilt her face so he could read her thoughts.

Why had he thought the sunlight was gone from the day, he wondered in growing, overwhelming, gut-catching relief. It was there in her yellow-sparked amber eyes. It was there, warming him all the way through with the heat of her understanding gaze. She had the power to forgive him, to let him forgive himself, and she was using it.

The fingers that held her jaw dove into the thickness of her hair to pull her face against his neck. He tipped his head back and blinked rapidly to clear the moisture from his eyes. Then he put his lips to the crown of her head, inhaling the clean beautiful scent of her. "Oh, God," he breathed roughly. "Oh, dear and blessed God. I love you, Samantha."

WITH THE ADVENT of a summer storm, the beach was almost deserted. But Max and Samantha walked arm in arm, facing into the wind, reveling in its strength. Their relationship, even in its infancy, had weathered a worse storm and survived.

She looked up at his profile. He wore the calm assurance of a man who has finally come to accept the things he cannot change. She wasn't fool enough to think that she had helped to erase his guilt. As he'd said, he would always have it. But he could live with himself now.

She had learned more about Max than he realized, and she had to wonder at the scope of this man's character. He expected more of himself than any ordinary mortal should be expected to, and he had felt that he'd betrayed his talents. He must learn to make mistakes like the rest of humanity. If he was not a man of integrity he wouldn't have felt the weight of his guilt so heavily.

She would be eternally grateful that her reaction had been the right one. She hadn't consciously analyzed her response, but had let her feelings dictate her actions. When he'd turned to her with that lost expression in his eyes, she'd wound her arms around him and held on tightly, trying to absorb some of his pain into her own slender body. There was no need for words, not at that time.

A drop of wetness touched her cheek. Was she crying now, when the tension had been relieved? Another drop hit her forehead and her nose, and all at once the clouds opened up.

Max came to a stop and looked to the sky before meeting her eyes ruefully. "We're going to get soaked," he said.

"I don't care." She turned her face up, too, and stuck out her tongue for a taste. When she met his loving gaze it was with a mischievous smile. "Unless you're afraid you'll ruin your glamorous tuxedo pants. My shorts can take it." She had on a pair of cutoffs and a sweat shirt that had certainly seen better days.

Max had rolled up the black pants to his knees, baring his muscular calves, and was still wearing the pleated shirt. The sleeves were characteristically turned back over his forearms, and the tails flapped in the breeze. She thought he looked as handsome as a matinee idol and wonderfully masculine.

He shrugged. "Suits me. But if you'd just let me go home to change..." he complained, trying to look very put out.

She took a half step to face him and put a finger in the shallow cleft in his chin. "Who's stopping you?" she chided, but gently. He was still tender from the emotional upheaval he'd just gone through. Physical activity should release some of his tension.

He caught her closer in a bone-crushing embrace, lifted her toes from the sand and whirled her around once before setting her on her feet again. "I don't want to spend a second apart from you today. Why won't you go with me? Are you afraid Abe and Anna will know we spent the night together?"

"Not really," she answered after a moment of hesitation. Was she? Nonsense, she was a grown woman. She raised her face to the rain again. "We'll go later. I just want to walk on the beach in this wonderful storm."

He laughed. "Only you would call a storm wonderful."

"But it is," she corrected, raising her voice over the sound of the wind. "It's glorious! The rain isn't cold and I want to walk with you."

The wind had picked up quickly. He brought her back into the shelter of his arms and bent his head to be heard. "It's been a long time since I walked in the rain, darlin', but I want to do everything with you." His lips lingered at the sensitive lobe of her ear to nibble.

She laughed lightly and pulled away. "Your mustache tickles!" she laughed. She danced toward the curling surf. "I'll race you," she called and began to run.

Max watched her for a moment, in fascination and wonder. Then he threw off the mantle of depression, of sorrow and guilt and began to run, too. He felt blood pumping, churning through his veins with life-giving, driving power, the strain on the muscles of his calves and thighs as he ran. He felt the rain pelt his skin and the wind tear through his hair and whistle in his ears. He felt all those things and was glad to be alive.

He caught and passed her in a flash and turned to run backward. "Show-off!" she yelled, and put on all her speed, passing him again. After a long time of toying with her, letting her get ahead and then passing her with consummate ease, he veered and ran toward her with purpose in his eyes, but she dodged.

They were both breathless when he finally caught her around the waist. Her legs and arms still churned in a parody of a run. "Let me down, you brute! You're just afraid I'll win!"

"No chance—!" He laughed. "Your legs are too short!"

"Then you can just carry me all the way home," she informed him loudly, wrapping her arms around his waist and her legs around one of his. She hung on to his side rather like a small monkey.

He made a dramatic show of limping, which had her laughing so hard that she forgot to hold on. She hit the wet sand on her backside. "O-w-w."

"Poor baby," Max consoled, scooping her up in a more conventional carry against his chest. They were both soaked and his hands slipped.

Samantha squealed. "Don't drop me again!" His arms tightened until she was no longer precarious in his hold.

Little did she know that he would never drop her, never let harm of any kind come to her, as long as there was breath and strength and life in his body to prevent it.

Samantha let her head rest against his shoulder, her breath coming in small gasps. Max was not even breathing hard, darn him.

"Did you bruise your little tush?" he crooned in her ear.

She wound her arms around his neck. "Yes, and it's all your fault. What do you suggest as a remedy?" she asked with a suggestive wink.

He grinned down at her. "I'm sure I can think of something."

She was so captivated, so thrilled at the sight of him laughing, grinning after the torment she'd seen in his eyes such a short while ago, that she forgot to answer. The rain blurred her vision, or was it tears?

His footsteps slowed, stopped. He held her gaze with infinite tenderness. "You are very good for me, Dr. Hyatt. It did help. It helped a lot."

"I'm glad," she said very softly, but he heard.

He lifted her higher in his arms and covered her lips in a kiss as tender as his smile. "The horseplay helped, too."

"The running," she corrected, "was for me. I haven't been getting any exercise lately and sitting at that piano for four and a half hours at a stretch leaves me stiff and tired."

He looked innocent except for the slight tilt to his mustache. "Well, I've shown you the remedy for stiffness and tiredness, haven't I?"

THEY SHOWERED TOGETHER under hot water, but its temperature couldn't begin to rival the heat of their bodies. They dried each other slowly with deliberate arousing caresses, until they were wild with desire. And then they spent the remainder of the day in bed.

8

"WHERE WOULD YOU LIKE to go for dinner?" Max asked, shifting his large body until they lay nose to nose. He touched her swollen lips with his and smiled contentedly.

She stretched like a sleek satisfied cat, and curled her arms around his neck. "I don't know. Where would you like to go?" Then suddenly she unwound herself and sat up. "Yes, I do know. I want to go the Oyster Bar and hear Johnny and the Rural Route."

Max rolled onto his back and watched her, amusement clear in his eyes. "Are you sure?" he asked, linking his hands behind his head. "It's not the tamest spot in Destin, even on Sunday night."

"Oh, but I'm not afraid. I have the perfect bodyguard for a place like that." She lifted the heavy weight of her hair off the back of her neck. The action raised her breasts and she noticed that Max couldn't seem to look anywhere else. It was strange, this feeling of being totally comfortable and actually enjoying her nudity.

Max finally cleared his throat and swallowed hard. "I won't let anything happen to you," he agreed huskily.

She dropped one arm to poke a finger in his ribs.

"I didn't mean you," she teased. "I meant the star. Johnny invited me to come anytime."

Max gave a growl and pulled her down to pin her body under his length. "*I* will take care of you," he said firmly.

Samantha was surprised that she didn't take offense at the pronouncement. She'd never particularly enjoyed being the object of a man's protective instincts. Now Max was watching her closely, waiting for a reaction, probably assuming that she would protest. She decided to fool him.

"I'm relieved. You know, Johnny is really just a boy, and I'll feel much safer with a big strong man to protect me." She kept her face straight and her eyes innocently wide, though it wasn't easy with him looming over her, watching like a hawk for a break in her sincere facade.

A reluctant half smile finally floated across his lips. "Liar," he accused gently. "You're the most self-sufficient lady I know."

Did that bother him, she wondered as he moved away to let her sit up.

"I'll have to go by the hotel to change. I'm not going to the Oyster Bar in a tux, even one that looks as bad as that one." He eyed the rumpled pants she had spread over the chair to dry.

"I am sorry that it's ruined. You looked so handsome in it."

He stood, giving her a careless grin over his shoulder. "I have another. I only hope the pants haven't shrunk so much that I can't get them zipped."

He got them zipped, barely, but the cuffs were well above the ankles. The doorman looked properly horrified when they reached Sea Tangle. They held their laughter until they were behind the doors of the elevator.

OVER THE PAST YEAR Max's room at the hotel had begun to take on some of his personality. As he saw it through Samantha's eyes, however, he realized how sterile it looked. *She should have seen it the first year,* he told himself wryly. He had not even sent home for his clothes. He'd bought a few pairs of jeans and some shirts and underwear. That was all he had needed.

He probably would still be wearing those same clothes if Anna hadn't ordered him to get a suit. "It's disgraceful, Max," the older woman had said. "You can't even go into the dining room with us for a decent meal."

He'd argued, but she was adamant. "And you get someone to send your golf clubs from home. Abe needs some exercise. You'll have to play with him."

He'd been touched by her concern. "This is home, Anna," he'd told her.

She'd swallowed with difficulty, but fixed him with a hard stare and proceeded to deliver a lecture that scorched his eardrums. "You're not doing anyone any favors wearing that hair shirt, and if you don't straighten up I'm kicking you out," she concluded.

Max knew it for the empty threat it was, but nevertheless he straightened. Now the clubs rested in the corner and a tennis racket was propped behind the door. He'd had one of his sisters pack his clothes. She'd done it grudgingly but thoroughly, sending far more than he'd ever wear. She had sent his stereo and albums, a television set, even his skis. She'd also included some of his law books. Most of the things were in storage in the basement of the hotel, but Anna had made him bring the books up to his room.

"We may need legal advice and we might as well get it free," she told him. She ordered the bookshelves herself and brought in some of her own plants in an effort to make the room more homelike. "A year is long enough to mourn," Anna had told him firmly. "We are going to get on with our lives now, Max, and that includes you."

SAMANTHA ROAMED the room while he showered. It was a standard hotel room, maybe a little more luxury in the furnishings than most, and spotlessly clean. She had an idea that the cleanliness was not because of the efforts of a hotel maid. There were no pictures, no personal mementos of any kind. The only books were law books, and on the bedside table, her copy of *Psychology for Today's Life-style*.

She sat on the edge of the bed and ran her hand over the neatly tucked spread. The room made her sad with its neatness, as though Max couldn't indulge himself at all, couldn't throw a dirty pair of jeans in the corner, couldn't crumple a piece of paper on the desk.

THE OYSTER BAR was in full swing when they entered. The noise hit her eardrums like a wall. Samantha peered through the haze of cigarette smoke but didn't see an empty table anywhere.

From his superior height Max spotted a table in a dimly lit corner and guided her through the crowd with a hand at the small of her back. She was grateful for its warmth. The customers were mostly male and she surmised that the beer had been flowing freely for some time now.

Johnny and the Rural Route was certainly popular. Foot-stomping, hand-clapping, shrill-whistle popular! She'd never seen such enthusiasm in an audience.

Max smiled at her wondering expression. "They'll be in Nashville recording top hits in a year or two." He had to shout to be heard over the clamor as the band wound up the number.

She grinned and nodded. When a sweating, smiling Johnny announced a break the noise dropped to a reasonable level and she could speak. "Just think. If I could have sung 'ba-beh' instead of 'ba-bee' I could be going with them."

He smiled again and reached for her hand. He didn't have to say anything. His thoughts were plain. *And we might never have met.*

The idea was unexpected and frightening enough to cause an involuntary tightening of her fingers around his.

Her reaction lit a blaze in the blue eyes. "Samantha...."

"Whatcha havin', folks?" The man wore the same kind of apron that Max wore when he was working, but the comparison ended there. His apron strings strained to reach around a gigantic belly, and the cloth was clean but marked with the stains and scorches of many wearings. A cigarette dangled precariously from his lips. He touched the point of the pencil to his tongue—Samantha held her breath waiting for the smoking cigarette to fall—before posing the pencil over a green pad that looked lost in his huge paw.

"Two pounds of boiled shrimp," Max told him without consulting Samantha. Then he added, "Do you have any crab claws?"

The man wrote diligently on the pad before answering. "Fresh this morning." One red-rimmed eye narrowed against the column of smoke that drifted from his cigarette toward the ceiling.

"Okay. One draft and...what do you want to drink, Samantha?"

"I'll have—"

The man's bored expression vanished immediately. He interrupted, an undertone of excitement in his voice. "Samantha? Are you the Samantha that tried out for the band?" He pulled the cigarette from his lips, dropping it on the wooden floor to be crushed by his heel.

"Well, yes, I—" She wasn't allowed to finish. Her hand was suddenly swallowed in the man's and pumped vigorously.

"I thought you must be. I ain't never known nobody else named Samantha before. Johnny told us to be on the lookout for you. What're y'all doin' at this dinky little table back here? Johnny'd skin me alive if he saw you off in a corner somewheres. Come with me."

With that he took Samantha's arm and hauled her bodily to her feet. Not that he was rough. On the contrary, he handled her like a feather, but his determination was dauntless.

"No really...it isn't necessary...we're fine where...." She looked back over her shoulder at Max, who was having a hard time controlling a grin. Shrugging his shoulders, he let the smile spread over his face and light his eyes with genuine amusement as he got to his feet and followed in their wake.

When they reached the edge of the dance floor, the waiter looked over the tables, deciding which was the best for the honored guest. Then, when he had chosen, he ordered the two men who sat there up and out with only a jerk of his beefy thumb!

"This here's a friend of Johnny's and he wants them right in front," he commanded.

"Oh, no! Please, I don't want to take these gentlemen's table!" Samantha said in horror. As big as he was, they were each approximately the same size as Max, and seemed about as complex as the man who held her arm. If they took offense, Max wouldn't stand a chance of protecting her, or himself, either.

But to her stunned surprise the two burly men rose without hesitation and the older one gave her a friendly, if overenthusiastic, pat on the shoulder.

"Sure!" he said cheerfully. "Any friend of Johnny's—"

Gallantly he held the chair for her, and she subsided gratefully into it. "Th-thank you." She managed a weak smile.

"No problem," said the younger man lightly. He lifted his hand in a companionable salute, nodded to Max, and the two of them shouldered their way through the crush of people, parting them as easily as Moses parted the Red Sea.

"Whew!" she said when Max had pulled a chair around next to her.

He laughed out loud. "You were absolutely right about your bodyguard. I won't ever worry about your being taken care of at the Oyster Bar. Those roughnecks metamorphosed into perfect gentlemen with one look from your golden eyes."

She dimpled. "They were nice, weren't they? But it wasn't my eyes. It was Johnny's doing."

At that moment Johnny appeared from a small door to the side of the stage. He waved and started wending his way toward their table. He had a firm hold on an equally delighted Jenny. After only a few delays to speak to his loyal fans, they made it and collapsed in the chairs opposite Max and Samantha.

"This is great, Miss Hyatt! I didn't expect to see you here so soon." He grinned in that slow way she remembered. "You got the job, huh?"

"I sure did, Johnny, and I want to thank you for telling me about it; but you neglected to mention I would be working with your wife."

"Did I?" The grin slid to Jenny and she responded with a rosy blush.

He laughed, but Samantha noticed that he didn't release Jenny's hand even to pour from the pitcher of beer that had magically appeared in front of them. It was sweet to see two young people who were so much in love. They probably were childhood sweethearts. She knew from her research that such marriages were often stable and strong from the very beginning. Boy and girl had gone through the stages of love as they were growing up and knew everything about each other long before they were married.

The waiter had only delivered three of the frosty beer mugs, and now he leaned down to ask Samantha respectfully if she'd like a Coke.

She looked at him blankly. "A what?"

"Well, Miss Samantha—" he dried his palms on his apron, leaving a few new streaks "—you don't look like the kind of lady who drinks beer."

"I don't?" She was even more amazed. She wondered what kind of lady she looked like. "But my friends are drinking it," she offered hopefully.

The man frowned. "Yes, and Jenny Worley knows that I don't hold with her drinkin' it, either. But Johnny's already corrupted her." He shrugged as though to say he'd done his best. If Jenny was going to drink beer, it was a crying shame, but he couldn't be blamed.

Max choked slightly and turned away, missing Samantha's warning glare. "I, uh, I think I will have a Coke, thank you," she told the man feebly and kicked Max under the table.

The man nodded, satisfied. "I'll bring your shrimp and claws right out."

Max could hardly contain his laughter until the waiter was out of earshot. It erupted and rolled over them like a tide, spreading to the nearby tables. The people who sat there smiled in appreciation of the big man enjoying himself so thoroughly. Johnny and Jenny joined in.

"You're a coward," Max gasped, wiping his streaming eyes. "The very practical Dr. Hyatt is a spineless coward!"

"I'm not," Samantha denied heatedly. And then a rueful smile curved her lips. "Well, maybe a little bit of a coward."

Max didn't relent. "Nope. A full-fledged, card-carrying coward is what you are. But I love you anyway." He bent forward to touch her lips firmly with his.

It was Samantha's turn to blush, a thing she never did. But Jenny's delighted smile and Johnny's hearty laugh provoked the surge of heat before she knew it was happening.

"I knew it," Jenny said with certainty. "I've seen

the way Max looks at the women he dates." She halted suddenly, glancing at Samantha in chagrin.

Including your sister, Samantha guessed, but she simply smiled.

"I knew there was something special between the two of you the first day," Jenny finished lamely.

"So did I," said Max softly. He still filled her vision and she couldn't, didn't want to, look away. They shouldn't be going public with this thing, not yet. Thinking of all the explanations that would be necessary if things turned sour, she shuddered. Within the next five minutes she would be willing to bet that Max was going to use the word *we* in connection with something they'd done. She could only hope he was discreet, she thought helplessly.

Johnny picked up his mug. "This calls for a toast. Maybe you could have just one sip of beer, Miss Hyatt...Dr. Hyatt? Did Max call you Doctor?" Johnny's voice rose on the question. Max's form of address had finally registered.

Samantha didn't want either of them to feel uncomfortable in any way because of her status. She hastily interjected, "Not a medical doctor. My doctorate only means that I went to school forever."

Johnny hesitated for a fraction of a second before he spoke. "I may be a red-neck but I know that a doctorate means a whole lot more than that," he said quietly.

She was stricken. Had she offended them anyway by trying to downplay the importance of her degree? She looked to Max for help but he was as much at a loss as she was. "I didn't mean—"

"I know. You didn't want to show off. You're a nice lady, Dr. Hyatt," said Johnny.

She breathed a sigh of relief but fixed him with a mock frown. "Johnny Worley, my name is Samantha or Sam. I am not a doctor of anything right now. I'm a piano player. It's what I always wanted to be anyway. Maybe I traded the dream of a concert hall for a cocktail lounge, but I'm happy. So don't ever call me doctor again."

"Yes, ma'am," he said meekly.

Samantha wasn't fooled by the passive tone, but the waiter was. He heard Johnny's words and looked from one of them to the other. "She your mother or somethin', Johnny?" he asked as he deposited two plastic trays lined with ice and heaped with plump pink shrimp and wicked-looking claws in front of Max and Samantha.

Samantha sputtered and Johnny glowered at the man. "Does she look like anybody's mother, Tiny?"

The man's eyes ricocheted over Samantha. He smiled sheepishly. "No, she don't, do she? The cook's making fresh slaw. It'll be out in a minute. What else?" he asked himself as he scratched the big belly. He snapped his fingers and reached out to the next table to confiscate the basket of cellophane-wrapped crackers.

"Hey!" protested the man at the table. He got to his feet with a threatening lurch.

"Keep your shorts on." The waiter gripped the man's shoulder to sit him back in his chair. "I'll bring you some more, but these here's friends of Johnny's."

Samantha's breath stopped and started again. "I'm glad I'm a friend of Johnny's," she said dryly and reached for a shrimp. She cocked her head at Johnny. "Tiny?" she asked, and he laughed.

"Tiny's my greatest fan."

"Second greatest," said Jenny.

Samantha quickly stripped the shell from the shrimp and popped it into her mouth. "Mmm. This is delicious. I'm starved. We jogged on the beach this morning and haven't eaten since." She froze, the second shrimp dripping in her fingers. *We?* She'd expected Max to be the one to commit the indiscretion, but she'd done it herself. What was happening to her? Her hands started to shake and she grabbed for a handful of paper napkins, drying her fingers vigorously in an attempt to hide her agitation.

"Have you eaten?" Max asked the other couple. He missed the unraveling of her composure.

Jenny nodded, but Johnny reached for one of the crab claws on Max's tray and the nut cracker.

Max slapped his hand away with a grin. "I didn't mean you, pal. You're always hungry. I was asking Jenny."

Johnny ignored him and cracked the shell over Max's tray. "Tell me something, Miss...Sam. Why didn't you study to become a concert pianist? You're good enough."

Silently she held up a hand palm out and he nodded sagely.

Max and Jenny looked at them. "What?" they said in unison.

"My hands are too small for the demand of concert pieces," she explained. "It broke my heart when I quit growing. I am the same size now than I was at twelve years old."

"Twelve? My God!" Max exclaimed. "That makes me feel like a child molester!"

Jenny scowled at him. "Have you been molesting

this child, Max?" she asked. "When's the wedding?"

"As soon as I can get her to the altar!" Max answered without hesitation.

"I'm glad," Jenny told him sternly. "I'd hate to come after you with a shotgun!"

They all laughed, but Samantha's laughter sounded hollow in her ears. Wedding! Had he lost his mind? A picture formed in her mind, a picture of her hand with a band on the ring finger. The picture expanded to show that she was holding a baby in her arms, a baby with sandy-brown hair. She was the one losing her mind! Speculating on marriage and a family with a man she'd only known three days. Proceeding into this...relationship as though she had never studied behavioral science at all, just as though she'd never spent three years of her life conducting research on modern courtship, just as though she'd never written the book.

Conversation was sparse until the edge of Max's appetite had been dulled. As for Samantha, she had lost her appetite completely, but she kept peeling the shrimp before her.

When Johnny finished the crab he leaned back in his chair and pulled Jenny into the circle of his arm. He smiled reflectively and returned to the earlier subject. "Neither of our folks had the money to send us to college. As a matter of fact, when we get to Nashville, that's the first thing I'm gonna do, enroll my little Jenny in school."

"Only if you go, too," Jenny said pertly, looking up at him with so much love shining out of her eyes that it brought a lump to Samantha's throat. "You want it worse than I do."

He kissed the tip of her nose. "We'll see. Hey!" His mood did a quick turnaround. "We were about to drink a toast! To lovin'!" He raised his mug in salute and took a long deep swallow.

"To a potent overpowering emotion," Max added, tilting his glass, smiling tenderly at Samantha over its rim.

She hoped he wouldn't notice how weak her smile was but his eyes narrowed in suspicion. "You're awfully quiet all of a sudden," he said under his breath. When Johnny spoke she shrugged, grateful for the diversion.

"A toast to lovin' sounds better. A toast...a toast to lovin'," Johnny added softly to himself. A faraway look had darkened his eyes.

"Oh, no!' wailed Jenny. "Johnny, you promised! No songwriting on my night off." She turned to explain to Samantha. "He goes into a trance, won't speak to me, won't smile or *anything!* Max has seen him." She shook her husband's arm. "Johnny!" she protested hotly.

"Okay, honey," he said apologetically. "I got to get back to work anyway." He finished his beer off in two more deep swallows.

"Stay with us while we eat, Jenny," Samantha invited when Johnny had gone backstage. She wasn't ready for the explanations Max would demand when they were alone.

"If I wouldn't be in the way. I wouldn't want to...."

Samantha found a huge bowl of coleslaw in front of her. When had the man brought it? "You aren't interrupting anything. Max is rushing things a bit. We've only known each other for three days."

Avoiding his eyes she pushed aside some of the ice and helped herself to the creamy mixture, piling it on the edge of the tray.

"Four days and eight hours," Max corrected blandly, taking the bowl from her. He earned an amazed glance from Jenny.

Mentally Samantha counted. He was right. He met her wondering stare with an innocent smile before turning to Jenny. "I'm the only romantic in this love affair."

Jenny laughed, apparently willing to overlook his choice of words, to Samantha's great relief. She wasn't feeling guilty, she told herself, and it wasn't an affair...yet. In this day a woman who *didn't* have an affair was considered suspect, but theirs was just so...so quick! And she wasn't reacting the way she was supposed to, the way the cool and efficient Dr. Hyatt would have reacted.

Her thoughts drifted to the earlier conversation with Johnny. Wasn't that what she'd told him? She wasn't Dr. Hyatt, she was Samantha Hyatt, piano player, and who knew how Sam Hyatt, piano player, would react to anything? Sam Hyatt herself certainly didn't!

Into the path of her vision came a large hand. It took the peeled shrimp she'd been holding and directed it toward her face. Automatically she opened her mouth. She chewed slowly, contemplating, and when she had finished the morsel turned her head to meet his eyes.

"Are you okay?" he asked gently.

She nodded. *No,* she wanted to say. *No, I'm not okay. You are doing things to my peace of mind that I can't handle.*

At that moment the entire place seemed to erupt. The waiter was making his way slowly toward them from the swinging door of the kitchen. He raised the huge tray over his head to protect its contents and used his gigantic stomach as a battering ram to push people out of his way. "Sorry to bring your dessert before you've finished eatin', but we don't serve while Johnny's playin'." He deposited two huge pieces of pie on the table and swung away to answer a demand for a beer before the show.

Satisfied that for the moment she wouldn't have to do any heavy explaining to Max, Samantha relaxed in anticipation of enjoying the show.

Most of the crowd was on its feet, clapping and whistling with shrill piercing blasts. The noise level was even louder than when they first arrived.

Samantha noticed that some of them had to use the little fingers of both hands in the corners of their mouths; but others seemed to be able to accomplish the same sound by a strange contortion of their lips.

Johnny's lazy drawl, amplified by the microphone, quieted the crowd immediately, and Samantha's attention swung to the bandstand. The keyboard man, as Johnny had referred to the position the day she'd auditioned, was older than the other members of the group. He had a balding spot on top, and as they began to play she noted with satisfaction that she was a better piano player. But when the man opened his mouth to sing, her self-satisfied smirk disappeared. The man's hearty tenor voice was beautiful. And "country."

Before the first song was finished, she knew instinctively what Johnny had meant that day when he told her she just "wasn't country." And the reason had little to do with the way she pronounced the words or what she wore.

The Rural Route finished one piece and went into another. Samantha became aware that this music was a feeling, an emotion springing from the heart; words couldn't describe the mosaic character of the sound. Another song followed and Samantha was entranced. Pathos and humor, passion and grief, tenderness and despair, all the emotions of the human psyche were encompassed in the lyrics and music.

Never had she sat down with the deliberate intention of listening to country music. She'd heard it, of course. On the radio, on television, the popularity of the Nashville sound was indisputable. And Johnny's band must typify the best of it all.

When she wasn't looking at her husband, Jenny watched Samantha's growing fascination with an amused smile. "He's wonderful, isn't he?" she asked during a lull. "I knew from the moment I saw him he was on his way to the top. I was one of his groupies," she admitted shyly.

"You were?" Samantha was surprised. "I thought the two of you had probably grown up together. You seem so close."

Jenny laughed. "Oh, we are close, but I've only known him since Christmas."

"See, darlin'," Max put in. "The 'love zap' theory strikes again."

Jenny looked confused, but mercifully Johnny began the next song before Samantha was forced to try to explain.

THE TWO COUPLES left the bar together shortly after midnight. As they parted in the parking lot, Samantha turned to Johnny. "We'll be back. I really enjoyed your kind of music, Johnny. Even if I can't sing it."

"Great," Johnny answered. "And I'm coming to hear you play tomorrow night, Sam. Monday's my night off. Jenny tells me you're real good, but I have to see for myself."

Samantha was ridiculously pleased by the compliment. "See you tomorrow then." She actually had to choke back the "we'll" that belonged at the beginning of that sentence.

Max helped her into the front seat of his car and came around to get in himself, but he didn't start the engine immediately. "I have a feeling I'm not going to be invited to spend the night," he said grimly.

Her answer was quiet. "No."

"Sam, what the hell happened in there? One minute we were having a good time and the next all the light seemed to go out in you as though I'd pulled a switch. What did I say?"

"It wasn't anything." She tried to dismiss the subject, but Max wouldn't be diverted.

"Was it the mention of marriage? Babe, even *I* know that it's too soon for that kind of decision. I plan to give you at least another week." He tried to grin but didn't quite succeed.

"Oh, no, Max," she contradicted. "It isn't you, it's me." Her hand waved a helpless arc. "I don't know what's happening, but I know it's throwing me into total confusion. I…I need some time. Alone. Please. I realize that I'm not very romantic…. I'm not quite willing to consider the world lost for love…."

"Is that what's bothering you?" he interrupted. "I told you, darlin', it doesn't matter. I love you just like you are."

"That isn't all of it. I'm disturbed and upset. Do you realize that I said 'we'?"

At his blank look she twisted her hands together. She couldn't even explain with any degree of rationality. "I have to get my thoughts in order." She straightened her posture from its defensive slump to square her shoulders. "I have to decide how to proceed from this point on. Four days and eight hours is not long enough to decide whether to put your happiness in the hands of another person. You could hurt me, Max, more than I've ever been hurt before, and I have to decide if it's worth the chance."

"Twelve," he answered abstractedly.

"What?" She looked at him, but he was staring through the windshield.

"Twelve hours," he explained offhandedly. "Would you like to know what I think, Samantha?" he asked, turning to her. She nodded. "I think you're afraid of your own feelings. You hide behind a textbook to keep from admitting vulnerability into your life."

She started to interrupt, to tell him that she wasn't hiding at all, just being practical. Heaven knew, somebody had to be practical about this relationship, and he certainly wasn't.

He held up a hand to forestall her objection. "But I'm going to go along with your timetable for now, Samantha. Maybe you're even right. Maybe we do need more time, and I'm willing to give it to you."

"How big of you," she answered sharply, really nettled by his magnanimous offer.

"I only hope we don't lose something very special by rationalizing it to death."

Those had been her own thoughts this morning as she had watched the adolescents on the beach. Or was that yesterday? The phrase kept repeating itself in her brain as she readied herself for a night that promised to be very wrong. No, no, not wrong... long! Were even her thoughts going to be filled with Freudian slips?

9

MONDAY HAD BEEN A DIFFICULT DAY, thought Samantha crossly as she looked at herself in the mirror on Saturday morning. But as a matter of fact, so had Tuesday, Wednesday, Thursday and Friday.

She had a sneaking suspicion that Max had not only read her book, but had become an expert in the field of personal relationships. She could not fault his affection. He was loving, tender and solicitous to a maddening degree—exactly like the picture she had painted in her book of the perfect man.

He made beautiful love to her, controlled and infinitely patient, with no demands for sex. She knew the desire was there, of course, but the chapter that warned sex could cloud rational thinking might have been written by Max!

The only pressure he exerted was in his repeated request that she marry him; and that was her problem.

The claustrophobic feeling that gripped her at the thought of a permanent commitment was getting worse. Combined with the alien feelings of frustration, or rather in contrast to them, the situation was becoming unbearable. With Gregory, who had been her only other lover, she hadn't had this reaction. She'd never had it with any of the men she'd dated. Was it because unconsciously she'd always known there was no possibility of permanency there?

Something had to be done and soon. Not one to turn away from a problem Samantha tried to analyze the feeling and come up with a solution. But something kept getting in the way, something similar to a daydream, sending her thoughts on a circular merry-go-round pattern instead of the careful line of straight reasoning that was the normal characteristic of her thought process.

She had to admit to Max's romantic ingenuity. When she had arrived at the hotel a little early on Monday, by arrangement with Anna, he was not behind the bar. Alone in the room she wandered over to the window to look out to the beach and did a double take. Children played at the edge of the surf. Couples walked hand in hand along the rise of the dunes, and carved in the sand directly below the window, in letters ten feet long, were the words MARRY ME, SAM.

From behind her came a deep husky chuckle. "I'm glad you finally got here. The tide's coming in." Max's strong arms circled her from behind. She felt his warm breath in her ear. "In a few minutes all my hard work will be washed away."

Samantha resisted the urge to melt against him. Firmly she disentangled herself. "And what a shame that would be," she said, trying to keep the sarcasm out of her voice. Ignoring the request written in the sand took a major effort but she gave it a try, moving a step away and speaking brightly. "Anna is bringing Janie in a few minutes. I'm going to play for her to see if she responds to music."

Max slid his hands into the back pockets of his

jeans and nodded. "Sounds like a good idea," he agreed easily, but his gaze was sharp. "Samantha, you haven't answered my question."

"Question? You mean out there?" She waved a hand toward the beach.

He nodded somberly.

Her eyes took on a glitter of hardness. "It looks more like a demand to me. I told you, Max, I am not looking for a permanent commitment. The thought of marriage smothers me."

"I'm not giving up, darlin'. And I'm not planning to put you in bondage."

He was too serious. She forced her voice to a bright indifference. "Well, I must say, Max, you're imaginative."

She felt like she was under a microscope, those blue eyes studying her, looking for a chink in the armor of some particularly interesting insect. She was proud that she managed to keep the subject to innocuous topics until Anna arrived a short while later with Janie.

Just before Max turned to greet them Samantha noticed a twinkle in his eye aimed directly at her, proof enough that he'd recognized her evasive chatter for what it was.

He spoke quietly to the child while she and Anna greeted each other. "It's very good of you to take this time with Janie," the owner's wife said, still with the slight hint of reserve Samantha had noticed when they first met.

"I'm delighted," returned Samantha. "Children make the best audiences." When she'd called Anna earlier she'd explained briefly about her background in psychology, not wanting the woman to be anxious.

Now Anna looked at her quizzically. "I hope you won't take this the wrong way, Samantha, but you're not at all like the other psychologists who've worked with Janie."

Samantha laughed, acknowledging the blue silk tunic she was wearing. "I'm not exactly dressed for work," she agreed. "You should have seen me before I moved to Destin. I always wore what my superiors considered the proper professional image for my career: white coat, a pair of horn-rimmed glasses that I didn't need, and my hair twisted into a bun."

"Do you mind if I ask why you chose to give up your profession?"

"Of course I don't mind," Samantha answered, sincerity warming her voice. "You have a right to ask if you're going to trust me with Janie." She took a breath, but was not as hesitant to share her feelings as she thought she would be. "I thought I was in love and it didn't work out, and right after we broke off our relationship my father died. Those two things coming so close together made me take a long look at my life and I didn't like what I saw. I decided it was time for a change."

"I didn't mean to pry," said Anna softly. "I hope I haven't brought up any unhappy memories." The reserve was gone now, replaced by kindness and gratitude in the woman's eyes. She turned to where Janie stood sipping a soft drink that Max had fixed for her. "Janie, come here, sweetheart. Do you remember Samantha who plays the piano?"

"Hi, Janie. Bring your drink over if you like and I'll play some songs for you." Samantha's voice was low and gentle.

Janie didn't answer—Samantha hadn't expected

her to—but the brown-button eyes skittered to the instrument. Samantha walked over to take her place at the keyboard, leaving Janie to follow or not. The point was not to push, but to invite.

She struck a playful chord. "Let me see. When I was about your age one of my favorite songs was 'Lavender Blue.' Do you know the words? I think I can remember them." She smiled over her shoulder and launched into the traditional tune.

Janie clung to her grandmother's skirts while Samantha played two other lighthearted songs. Then the child's curiosity got the better of her. She ventured to the edge of the piano to watch as Samantha's hands flew over the keys.

Over the child's head Samantha nodded encouragingly to Anna, and the woman tiptoed quietly away. A few moments later Janie looked around for her grandmother. When she found Anna gone she tensed. Samantha held her breath but kept playing and talking, and in only seconds the stiffening in the small body relaxed.

Anna came back for Janie when it was time for the bar to open. Samantha was surprised how much she had enjoyed playing the old pieces for the child. She had not counted on a response—therapy was a long involved process—and she got none. Children's problems were not her specialty, but wouldn't it be exciting if she could get results with music where others had failed using more conventional methods?

"Thank you, Samantha. This has been a treat for Janie."

Samantha walked to the entrance with them. "And for me, Anna. It is absolutely no problem at all for me to come in to work thirty minutes earlier. If you want me to continue, that is."

"Every day?" asked Anna.

"No, it will be more effective if Janie doesn't see me every day. If she gets pleasure from the music she will begin to anticipate our sessions. Why don't we start with twice a week, say Mondays and Thursdays, and then move to three times a week in about a month or so if we see that it's helping."

"Fine. Then we'll see you on Thursday." Anna walked away, talking in an animated way to the little girl.

Samantha had to swallow past the lump in her throat before she returned to the piano.

"That was a very nice thing to do, Sam."

She looked up at Max, unable to speak for a minute. He smiled his understanding and lifted her chin with a finger to plant a soft kiss at the corner of her mouth. "I'll buy you a steak after work," he murmured.

"Okay," she said softly, nodding. "Will you stay off the subject of marriage?"

He sighed and shook his head. "For tonight. You drive a hard bargain, Dr. Hyatt."

"I know," she admitted. Then she remembered something. "Johnny and his group are coming tonight," she reminded him.

Max groaned. "That's right. Well, I'll buy steaks for Johnny and Jenny, too, but not for that drummer who keeps eyeing you like a nice juicy tidbit he'd like to sample."

A teasing smile tugged at her lips. "I didn't think you'd noticed."

"I notice everything that concerns you, darlin'.

Especially another man," he growled softly. "I'll have Jenny get rid of him."

The Rural Route came in about seven o'clock. Samantha didn't recognize them at first. Wearing sport coats and suits and ties, they looked like little boys tidied up for Sunday school. To her surprise they really seemed to enjoy her show.

Bearing a tray of foaming mugs, Max approached their table and she heard him say, "On the house." The group greeted him good-naturedly, even the drummer. After that the evening seemed to take on an additional sparkle.

Samantha sat with them during her next break, and when it was time to go back to the piano she urged the new keyboard man to join her.

Max came over at that moment and added his encouragement. "As long as you keep your hands on the piano and off my girl," he threatened with a grin.

They played several hilarious duets, much to the delight of the customers in the lounge. The next time Samantha looked at her watch it was almost nine-thirty. Max chased the remaining customers away with a vague promise to see about a repeat performance.

Everyone ended up at Samantha's apartment, including the drummer, to eat the steaks Max had purchased on the way. Obviously quite a bit of planning had gone into what gave the impression of an impromptu party, because Jenny arrived with a huge bowl of green salad and some crusty French bread.

Guitars harmonized with the piano after the dishes were stacked in the sink, and Samantha learned to play her first country song at Max's request. Although his features were blandly innocent, the devilish gleam in his eye gave him away when he asked for "Whatever Happened to Old Fashioned Love?"

The party broke up at 1:00 A.M. Max stayed only a few minutes after the others had left, just long enough to reduce her to a state of quivering jelly with a few very effective kisses.

Tuesday night he took her to a quaint French restaurant and over coq au vin had the strolling violinist play "*La Vie en Rose*." That night he left her at her door submerged in the same magic spell the song described.

Wednesday, Thursday and Friday she was subjected to more of the same. One morning he showed up at her doorstep at dawn to take her sailing. Another morning they walked the docks and had a huge breakfast at the pier. Max cooked his specialty for her one night—red snapper prepared in a brown paper bag. "You see what a good husband I'd make?"

She ignored the question but reached for another helping of the succulent fish.

Since they worked until nine, it was always after midnight before she got to bed, and she tossed and turned for hours before drifting into a restless sleep. The shadows under her eyes began to grow darker each day. But how could she fault him? He was doing everything according to her own book!

Saturday morning when she dragged herself out of bed to face the wreck in the mirror, she made up her mind that something had to be done. She certainly wasn't ready to accept a proposal of marriage. Possibly she never would be. But there was another answer. It would have to be carefully thought out because it was a big decision. Big? It was gigantic.

Weighing the pros and cons took most of Saturday morning. She wasn't one to do things halfway so she sat down at the table with pencil and paper. Drawing a line vertically down the middle of the page she began to list the advantages of her plan on the left side and the disadvantages on the right side. At the end of the exercise she still wasn't convinced she was doing the right thing.

However, she had moved here with the express purpose of changing her life to include some pleasure. This plan would definitely be pleasurable, very pleasurable indeed, but it could also be hazardous.

When she arrived at Sea Tangle on Saturday afternoon she marched directly to the bar before she could change her mind. "Max, I'd like to talk to you," she stated.

"Of course, angel," he agreed quickly. "Would you like to use the office?"

Angel? Yuk. The damn book again. "A woman enjoys the little things—affectionate terms of endearment, tender compliments, etc." Max had been heavy-handed with both all week. She loved it when he softly drawled "darlin'." And the typically southern "honey" and "babe" didn't bother her. But "angel" and "sweet" were too much.

She looked around. They were alone. "No, this will be fine."

He folded his arms on the bar and looked at her expectantly. She hitched a hip up onto the barstool much as she had done that first day, and faced him across the shining surface.

She had dressed with deliberation, was tempted to

wear the gold chain, but dismissed it as too obvious. She had chosen the strapless sundress she'd worn for her debut in the lounge. Max had seemed to like the dress after he was assured that it stayed up without visible means of support. It displayed her shoulders to advantage and molded closely to the curves of her breasts and waist. Its black-and-white print was a perfect foil for her shimmering auburn hair.

This was not going to be the easiest conversation she'd ever had, but she had to admit to a certain gleeful anticipation of his reaction. She schooled her lips not to twitch. "Would you like to move in with me?"

He didn't bat an eye. "Yes, I would," he answered easily.

She waited, but no further comment was forthcoming. "When?" she finally blurted.

He stroked his mustache, seeming to contemplate, and glanced at the ceiling. "We're both off tomorrow," he suggested.

She breathed a sigh of relief. The worst part was over. Her elbows met on the counter and she linked her fingers together. "That will be fine. Now, there are a few things—"

She was interrupted by a sharp snap of his fingers. "I forgot. The bartender that takes over the luncheon crowd on my day off is bringing his wife home from the hospital. She just had a baby. I promised Abe I would fill in for him." He smiled apologetically.

This wasn't working out at all as she had planned it. She was at a loss as to how to continue. "Well..." she said weakly. Her hands fell into her lap. Disappointment made her shield her eyes from him. Her head bent, sending a swath of hair forward over one shoulder. She slid off the stool and turned to go. "Whenever," she offered in what she hoped was a casual manner.

Suddenly she was seized from behind and lifted off her feet. He had come out from behind the bar like lightning and with the sneaky tread of a cat. His deep laughter vibrated against her spine as he nuzzled his face into her hair. "What about tonight?" He set her on her feet and she twisted around to look at him. When she saw the mischievous gleam in his eye, his grinning face, she aimed a fist at his stomach. But she had to admit to an overwhelming surge of relief at having the old Max back. The perfect man had become a bit wearing.

THE TOP WAS DOWN on the Mercedes and it was filled to overflowing. Samantha had to use the side mirror to see behind her as she drove because his skis protruded out of the area behind the front seat. "Skis?" she'd asked, unbelieving. Skis in Florida?

"You never know when you'll need something," he had answered blandly.

"You could always return to the hotel for them at the first sign of a snowstorm," she teased.

She had insisted that he leave some of his things in his room. They were going to do this by the book, and the book said to make the changes slowly, to keep two places for a while.

He had agreed, but then he had taken her down to the storage room in the basement and started filling her arms with an assortment of things it seemed he could no longer live without. The skis came under that category.

She shook her head, half in amusement, half in

exasperation, and maneuvered a difficult left-hand turn. Max was right behind her in his sedan.

She supposed this experiment would be all right. She'd never done this before—with Gregory she had never even contemplated their moving in together—but as long as she and Max followed the guidelines the transition should go smoothly.

In the office behind the bar, during her breaks, they'd discussed their motives. Or rather she'd discussed hers. His was clear and bluntly stated. He wanted to marry her. She wanted to be together for a while, to see how they got along in the new living arrangement.

Samantha was surprised when he didn't attempt to make love to her during those breaks. After all, this was a big step. He might act a bit more eager.

When the last of Max's things had been dragged up to the condominium and piled into the guest room temporarily, they collapsed on the sofa.

Now that they were here, now that he had actually hung some clothes in her closet, well, the guest-room closet—the book was adamant about separate closets—she was beginning to feel nervous.

She jumped to her feet and headed for the kitchen. "It's almost midnight. Are you hungry?" she asked brightly.

"Are you?"

She felt as if she would choke if she tried to eat anything. "Yes, I'm starved. But it's so late, how about just scrambling some eggs?" She opened the refrigerator door to peer inside.

He moved again on those cat feet and before she could avoid him he was behind her with one hand at her waist, looking over her shoulder. It was the first time he'd touched her in hours and the effect was electric. She jumped as if she'd been shocked.

Max looked down at her, understanding and tenderness in his blue eyes, and closed the refrigerator. "Sam, the kids have a word for it. Am I invading your space? Are you sorry already that you invited me to move in?"

She laid her head on his shoulder, slowly and carefully. "No. I'm not sorry. I suppose I'm nervous because I haven't lived with anyone since I moved out of my father's house, but I'm glad you're here," she said softly.

He was just as slow, just as careful, when he bent his head to cover her lips with his in a brief kiss. "Then could we put off the domesticity part until later?" he murmured. "I have a powerful need to make love to you."

She raised her arms to wind them around his neck. "You're new around here, but I believe you know your way."

The words seemed to release the restraint that had characterized all of his actions for the past week. With a muffled groan he swung her up into his arms and headed toward the bedroom with long impatient strides. His face was a study of hunger and desire as his eyes moved restlessly across her features. "For the past week I've been trying to keep my hands off you. Do you realize what that has done to me?" His whisper was thick and an expression of something resembling pain darkened the blue eyes to midnight.

"I wanted you, too, Max."

He reached the opened door to her bedroom. "Then why, for God's sake...?" He swallowed the rest of the question and covered her mouth greedily.

Her dress had a long zipper in the back. As soon as her feet touched the floor he reached around behind her to pull the slide down. In his haste he was clumsy and halfway down the tab caught in the fabric, refusing to release the tiny teeth any further.

Her arms were still wrapped tightly around his neck, her lips busy leaving kisses along his throat. When she finally realized what was happening she couldn't help the giggle that escaped. She was suddenly caught against him in a hard grasp, which emptied the air from her lungs.

"Samantha, do you like this dress?" he asked harshly.

"Uh-huh," she answered, more interested in the pulse that throbbed just underneath his clenched jaw. Her tongue snaked out to measure its beat, provoking a moan from deep within his chest, as she had known it would.

His fists closed on the sides of the zipper and wrenched it apart. She heard the fabric tear but at the moment she couldn't waste a regret on the cantankerous dress. *There must be some of the primitive animal in each of us,* she thought briefly before he stepped back to let the dress fall to the floor. And then all further thought was suspended.

She was as rough on his shirt as he had been on her dress. In only seconds they stood naked, both struggling to take in enough breath to maintain consciousness. Anxious hands caressed feverishly in restless agitation, reacquainting themselves with the soft curves and hard planes, the sensitive places that deserved a softer touch and the spots that were not content with a gentleness but demanded a stronger grasp.

Max followed her urging when she fell back onto the mattress and pulled him with her. When he entered her it was not the slow careful entry she'd known before, but a demanding thrust that expanded her horizons to a new and glorious plane. She responded to his need, expressing her own desire in an erotic rhythm as impassioned as his. Her nails gripped the muscles of his shoulders, and her hips arched upward to take more of him. "Max! Oh, God, Max," she cried at the moment of release, her body a trembling burst of convulsion that seemed to go on and on.

"My love, my love," he rasped as he stiffened for an endless minute and then shuddered with a force that left him drained and gasping.

After a moment to gain his breath, he looked down at her, concern scoring the lines around his eyes. "Did I hurt you, Samantha?" His shaking had stroked the hair away from her cheek and remained to cradle her head. "I didn't mean to be rough, but it's been so long. Oh, God, did I hurt you?"

"No, no." She turned her lips into his palm. "You didn't hurt me. It was wonderful. I've never known anything like that before."

His smile was tender and loving but rather rueful. "Neither have I, my darling." His lips feathered over her eyes, her cheeks, and reached for her mouth. "Neither have I," he whispered, his warm breath like a caress against her lips.

THE NEXT MORNING Samantha left Max asleep and slipped quietly into the kitchen. She was turning pancakes when he came out of the bedroom looking rumpled and sleepy and altogether wonderful.

"Good morning, my love," he murmured, kissing her on the side of her neck. "Do I have time for a shower?"

"If you hurry." She smiled.

"Five minutes," he promised.

Thirty minutes later the pancakes were like soggy rubber and the bacon was limp. But Samantha bit back an angry rebuke as she joined him at the table on the balcony. He looked refreshed and neat in his ordinary working clothes, the jeans that were only slightly faded and the crisp dress shirt with the sleeves folded back. She felt disheveled and grumpy from trying to keep breakfast warm and herself cool. She hadn't dressed.

Max raised a brow when he noted the condition of their breakfast, but he didn't say a word.

"Max, we must do some more talking when you get home. In order for us to get along well we must make some important decisions."

He sighed. "Darlin', you are going to talk this relationship to death," he said with a patient grin. "Okay, shoot."

"To begin with, Stage Two is a time of discovery, and if we are honest with each other now it will save a lot of conflict later when we reach Stage Three."

"I've read about Stage Three." Max nodded. "It doesn't sound like very much fun to me."

"Stage Three is the testing ground. That's when you find out that I'm an awful nag, or I find out that you're impotent."

"Samantha! Don't even *think* such a thing!" He tried to hide his grin but it wasn't necessary. She was laughing, too.

Then she sobered. "I know it seems like I'm asking

for trouble, but Stage Three is important. We have to find out if we can tolerate each other's foibles. We couldn't possibly make this thing permanent if we can't get through Three."

He looked hopeful. "Do you mean marriage?"

"You know I won't discuss marriage, Max. Right now we're in a fantasy, but when the realities set in we may not even like each other."

He didn't answer.

"Now." Samantha pulled a pad and pencil toward her. "First we must divide the chores."

"I'll cook," said Max.

"But I like to cook, too," she protested.

He looked dubiously down at his plate.

Squaring her shoulders decisively, she decided to be honest about her earlier annoyance. "You told me you'd only be five minutes in the shower. There was nothing wrong with the pancakes five minutes after you told me that."

"You should have waited until I was finished. You had those pancakes on the griddle when I went *into* the shower."

Samantha looked at him, horrified. "We're arguing already," she whispered.

Max got to his feet and came around the table to scoop her up in his arms. He carried her into the living room and sat down on the sofa with her in his lap. "There is nothing wrong with arguing, darlin', as long as we don't use the knife of personalities. We just had a disagreement. I imagine we'll have many of those, but they don't mean we care any less for each other, do they?"

Samantha snuggled her nose under his chin. "No," she answered.

"Now let me tell you what I want you to do."

She looked up.

"I want you to draw up the budget, a list of the chores and anything else you think we should discuss, while I go to the hotel. I should be back around two-thirty. We'll sit down and thrash all this out, okay?"

She nodded, surprised that he seemed to be taking over the organization of their living together. Wasn't she supposed to be the practical one? The book again, she realized. He was following the guidelines set out in her book. "You're trying to stay ahead of me again, Max."

He smoothed the hair away from her face and kissed her tenderly. "I know," he said quietly. "We've discussed motives, Sam, and I've been honest with you about mine. But you haven't been completely open about your own, have you?"

"I don't understand," she murmured.

"Don't you, darlin'? You keep warning me about all the bad things that you seem sure will happen to us." He paused. "I think you've asked me to move in with you in order to try to get me out of your system, Samantha. But I'm telling you right now that it won't work." He watched carefully for a reaction.

Samantha's eyes drifted to a point behind his head. Was that one of her motives? It was not one of the reasons she'd listed on the paper, but was it an unconscious one?

Suddenly she surged to her feet. He was putting her on the defensive, which was another way of pressuring her to do what he wanted. "That's a terrible thing to say. It makes me sound like some kind of emotional cripple who's using you. Just because I don't fall gratefully into your arms and accept your proposal you think I have ulterior reasons. Besides, it didn't take you very long to accept," she challenged.

He smiled and got to his feet in one lazy graceful motion. "About a quarter of a second if I remember correctly." Tucking his fingers into the back pockets of his jeans, he ambled toward her.

"I remember it that way, too," she snapped, trying to overlook the way the move molded his shirt to the broad chest and his jeans to his powerful thighs. "If you thought you were being used, why did you agree so quickly?"

Sudden laughter burst from him and he rocked slightly back on his heels. "Why do you think, you little idiot? I want you any way I can get you. If making myself indispensable around the house, if letting you become used to having me here will accomplish that in the end, then that's what I'll do. Did you really think that I would stand on some stupid principle and say if you won't return my love I won't let myself be used? My darling Samantha, you have my heartfelt permission to use me in any way, at any time you see fit!"

Samantha's jaw had dropped at the beginning of his speech. "But I don't want to use you," she muttered.

"Why should you mind if I don't?" he asked reasonably. He moved a step closer, forcing her to tilt her head back.

The now-familiar scent of the after-shave he wore drifted to her nostrils, and the languor she always felt when he was this close weighted her lids, sending them down to half cover her eyes. "I don't know.

It just seems sort of underhanded." Her voice became huskier. Her body swayed in his direction.

"Let me worry about it, okay?" His words seemed to come from somewhere deep within his chest, emerging with difficulty.

"All right, I'll let you worry," she whispered.

The tilt of his mustache warned her a second before his mouth opened over hers. His hands remained in his pockets but he took her weight as she leaned in to accept the kiss, her palms spreading on his chest. "Max...."

His mouth moved with practiced mobility and his eyes fell shut, but still he didn't hold her. Finally he drew back. "I have to go," he groaned, attempting to grin. "Hold that pose."

She chuckled weakly and forced her knees to accept all her weight again. "Yes, sir. May I have a shower and put on some clothes?"

Max pretended to ponder. "If you must," he finally acquiesced. "Just don't put on too many."

WHEN MAX RETURNED, it was closer to three. Samantha was in a huddled ball on the sofa, tears streaming down her face. The doorbell rang and she leaped to her feet, scrubbing her cheeks with the heels of her hands. "I'm so glad you're here," she told him and whirled away from his outstretched arms to return to her spot.

"Samantha, what's wrong?" He spoke over the sound of the television and followed to stand over her like some knight ready to slay dragons.

But he blocked her view. She pushed at his legs and waved feebly at the TV, a fresh wave of tears wetting her cheeks as effectively as the rain that poured down, washing away the ink on Humphrey Bogart's letter. All that remained were the poignant words at the end: "all my love, Ilsa."

"Damn, Samantha. You've got to quit doing these things to me." He sat down beside her on the sofa. Gathering her under his arm he reached for the huge yellow bowl on the coffee table. Silent except for the crunch of buttered popcorn, they watched the rest of the movie together. When the haunting theme played for the last time and Ingrid Bergman walked through the mist, away from her love forever, Samantha buried her face in Max's chest and wept anew. She missed the sudden gleam in his eyes as he looked tenderly down at her bent head. His arms tightened comfortingly.

The rest of the afternoon was spent arranging Max's belongings. They hooked his stereo and speakers to her tape player, giving themselves quadraphonic sound. They made room for his albums on the shelves, but his law books were another story. "We'll have to buy some more bookshelves, but where will we put them?" she asked him from her cross-legged pose in the middle of the rug.

Max hefted a couple of the heavy volumes. "I need a desk, too. Would it be all right with you, darlin', if I use the guest room as a kind of study? Abe would let us store the bed at Sea Tangle."

"Sure," she agreed readily. "If we have guests we can send them to the hotel. It's not that far."

"I'll go out in the morning to see what I can find," he said absently. "Or...."

"Or what?"

Dropping the two books back into the carton,he came down onto his haunches beside her. He looked thoughtful. "Is next Saturday your free weekend this month?"

"I don't know," she answered dubiously. "Abe never said which Saturday, and I haven't been working for a full month yet."

"If he agrees, would you like to go to Jacksonville? I have a desk and shelves that belonged to my grandfather at my house. They would fit in with your furniture. We could rent a truck and bring them here."

"I didn't realize you still had your house." She bit her tongue before she could ask the obvious question. Did he expect to return to it?

He shrugged and stood, catching her hands to bring her up with him. "When I left I closed it, but I wasn't sure at that point what I was going to do, so I didn't put it on the market." He linked his hands behind her bringing the lower half of their bodies together. "It probably would be a good idea to call a real-estate agent while we're over there."

Samantha had a rather unpleasant thought. "Didn't you tell me that you had a brother who lived in Jacksonville?"

"And two sisters. Are you afraid to meet my family?"

It was a deliberate challenge and he knew it. If she said yes she would be presenting herself not only as a coward but also as reluctant to pursue the next step in Stage Two: Going Public.

"I suppose I could... think about it."

"You have all week. I wouldn't want you to go if it would make you uncomfortable."

She wrapped her arms around his waist and let her head rest on his chest, listening to the regular heartbeat beneath her ear. She didn't know what to say.

His hand stroked the length of her spine and back up under the thick curtain of hair to her nape. "My folks *can* be pretty intimidating."

That was just the spur she needed. She wasn't easily intimidated. Not Dr. Samantha Hyatt. "Nonsense. I'd love to meet your family." She pulled a short distance away, but he wouldn't release her completely.

"There's just one more thing." He looked as though he wanted to appear embarrassed but didn't quite make it. Finally he gave up and a grin broke through. "How do I introduce you? As my mistress? Roommate? Lover? My family are pretty straightlaced, I'm afraid, especially my mother."

"I thought your parents spent their summers in North Carolina." Score one for the home team.

"They do, but I haven't been home for two years and I'm sure that my sisters will call them. They'll be there, if only to see if I've decided to return to the fold." A trace of bitterness crept into his voice.

"And have you?" Samantha asked softly.

"No, darlin', I haven't. I'll admit that I have given some thought to returning to law, especially since I met you."

"Me? Why?"

"It hurt to give up my career. I loved the law, Samantha, but for so long I felt unworthy. You have helped me to rationalize those feelings. I've done a little work for Abe and it's whetted my appetite. But if I do go back it will be on a much smaller scale than the law that Stanwood, Stanwood, Graham and Graham practice."

That statement provoked so many questions she didn't know which to ask first. She decided to start with the least important. "How did the Grahams get in there?"

"My older sister and her husband," he explained offhandedly before returning to the subject. "You give me thoughts and dreams of permanency, darlin'. I guess it's time to heal this rift with my family. Maybe if you help I can make them understand why it happened in the first place." He nuzzled her neck. "I want my children to have the best education I can give them—I certainly can't do that properly on a bartender's salary—and I want them to know their grandparents."

"Children? Max, you're going too fast again," she scolded, pulling free. "We are not getting married!" She stalked into the kitchen. "What do you want for dinner?" she demanded.

She knew it for the foolish question it was almost immediately, but too late for her to evade his arms as he swept her up and started down the hall.

Before she succumbed completely to the magic of his lovemaking she had one more question. "Max, why did you bring your skis?" she asked as he laid her tenderly on the bed.

"Because, Dr. Hyatt, just because," he said.

"But, Max...."

"I'm busy right now," he informed her as he stripped the T-shirt over her head. "Think about it. I'm sure you'll come up with the reason."

It was too hard to keep her mind on skis with all the interesting things he was doing to her with his hands and lips. "I'll think about it later," she told him.

10

THE TRIP to Jacksonville was distinguished by two rather startling revelations.

The first: Max's family members were treating his self-imposed exile about as seriously as if he was going through an adolescent stage. His abandonment of his career was merely annoying to them, a postponement, as it were. They obviously expected him to return to the fold in the very near future.

His efforts to convince them otherwise were met with indulgent amusement, which frustrated him to distraction. The picture of the vitally masculine and arrogantly assured Max Stanwood trying to hold on to his temper while explaining to his petite ladylike mother that she was mistaken if she thought he would ever return to the family firm, would have been funny if it hadn't been so disturbing.

And the second revelation was even more worrying to Samantha. Max's former fiancée was invited to join his family for the weekend celebration of the return of the prodigal son.

Not that she was jealous, not at all, Samantha told herself. Jealously was a demeaning emotion, unworthy of notice. It was just that the gorgeous glamorous lawyer was so...so tall. Her name was Lydia Stone, but there wasn't one thing hard about her.

Her smile, even through those intelligent eyes, was soft and appealing.

At odd moments Samantha found herself speculating about the way *their* bodies would fit together and the mental image hurt much more than she would ever have imagined. The only fault she could see in the woman was that Lydia seemed to share the assurance of his family that Max would eventually return to Jacksonville. Either Lydia didn't know Max very well or she, herself, didn't.

The only breathing space during the whole twenty-four-hour visit was when they went to Max's house to pick up the desk and bookshelves. The explanation as to why he needed the furniture could have been as sticky as his casual statement to his mother that during their stay they would need only one bedroom, but to Samantha's surprise no one questioned him.

"Conservative?" she whispered in an aside.

He lifted his brows and shrugged. "Beats me," he whispered back.

Even Lydia was blasé, which was more than Samantha would have been under the circumstances, she realized. If she had once been in love with someone and he had brought home another woman, she would have felt at least a trace of uneasiness. But Lydia was as charming and friendly as if they'd been friends for years. Samantha decided that it was for the best that the two of them had never married. Lydia wouldn't have been right for Max.

His house overlooked the Saint Johns River only a few blocks from his parents' home. While it wasn't as large as some of its neighboring estates, it was much too big for a bachelor, she thought as Max pulled into a circular driveway. The grounds around the house were beautifully maintained, and she wondered at that.

When he turned off the motor he sat for a moment looking at the imposing stucco structure. "It seems to belong to another person in another life," he murmured.

"The house is lovely, Max," she answered noncommittally. Was he feeling some of the pain and regret that had chased him from this place? She decided suddenly that she didn't like it here.

He folded his arms across the top of the steering wheel and leaned forward to look up to the roofline. "The house is a damn mausoleum, Samantha, and it holds the remains of a dead existence," he exclaimed bitterly. "Look at it! Does that pomp and pretension look like me?"

Her answer was careful. "No, not as you are now."

"And not as I would ever want you to see me," he said with heated sincerity. "I hate it. It's going on the market Monday. I don't know why I haven't sold it before this."

"Someone has kept the lawn mowed," she observed.

"There probably isn't a speck of dust in the place, either. You heard them. They think I'm coming home any day now."

Samantha stroked his back comfortingly. She couldn't think of a thing to say. Slowly under the touch of her fingers some of the tension in his muscles relaxed. He turned to smile at her over his shoulder. "Have I told you today that I love you?"

Her eyes met his, tenderness softening the amber

depths. "No, I don't believe you've mentioned it since last night," she said softly.

He released the wheel to draw her under one arm. The other arm circled her waist to pull her close. She shifted across the console wanting to be closer still and slid her arms around his waist. He inhaled the scent of her hair and burrowed his face in the curve of her neck. "I'm glad you're here with me," he whispered.

She was touched, deeply, by the admission. Her arms tightened. "We don't have to go in."

He raised his head, his eyes glowing with fondness. "You do have a warm heart, darlin'. The house holds no ghosts for me. I only meant that I'm glad you're here."

The kiss wasn't enough, wasn't nearly enough for either of them. Finally Max pulled his head back. "Why are we doing this in the car when there are plenty of beds inside?" he said hoarsely.

"Better yet...why don't we hurry and get the move over with so we can go home."

He pushed a curl behind her ear. "Do you know how good that sounds to me, my love?" He sighed. "Home."

He wanted her to see the things he planned to use, to approve them. Later he and his brother would load them onto a truck. They walked through the house hand in hand. It was lovely in a formal way, thought Samantha. Not at all the type of house she wanted, though. Children could never play in these rooms without putting the porcelains and collectible antiques in jeopardy; dogs and cats would have to be banished to keep them from shedding on the damask and velvet.

Children? What was she thinking of? Finally they arrived at a room that she loved. Obviously it had served as Max's study. The furniture they were taking back to Destin was in here, and she agreed, it would fit right into the condominium's decor. "I like it," she said.

"Good. This was my favorite room."

"Then you couldn't have been as much of a stuffed shirt as you described yourself. This room is comfortable. Why isn't the rest of the house like this?"

Max was embarrassed! She had never seen him embarrassed before. She watched, fascinated as heavy color rose to his hairline. "Well, uh...you see, Samantha...."

She decided to take pity on him. "Lydia picked out all the other things?" she asked casually.

"Yes." His answer was short and relieved.

"You don't have to worry about my feelings, Max. I am not a jealous person."

"You're not?"

Samantha laughed lightly. "Don't sound so disappointed. You wouldn't like it at all if I was. Jealousy makes people unreasonable and unpleasant."

"Oh, I don't know. I might like it if you were just a little jealous."

"I'm sorry." She spread her hands and shrugged. Then she spied the painting over the fireplace. "Oh, Max. I love this." It was a watercolor bright with the sunshine of a perfect day for sailing. Three boats were under full sail on the gray-green of the Atlantic Ocean. "Could we take it? It would look beautiful over the sofa."

"Sure."

Samantha hesitated. "Did, uh, did you choose this painting?"

"No, it was a gift," he said carelessly.

From Lydia. He didn't have to tell her. All at once she decided that she didn't like it as much as she had before. The colors really weren't *exactly* right. She tilted her head and looked at it again, dubiously. "Well...."

"My sister gave it to me, and you are jealous!" he hooted. He wrapped his arms around her waist, lifting her off the floor to plant a kiss on her surprised lips.

"I am not!" she protested, threading her fingers through the hair at his nape. "I just didn't want you to be uncomfortable having something around that your former girlfriend gave you."

Before he could comment she touched her tongue to his mustache and traced a path across his upper lip. Max forgot all about the subject of jealousy, as she'd known he would.

SAMANTHA WAS GREATLY RELIEVED when it was finally time to go back to Destin. She looked forward to the few hours alone in her car. Max would follow in the small truck they had rented to move the furniture.

Though the entire trip was accomplished on an interstate road and the little Mercedes practically drove itself, Samantha had a stiff neck and a raging headache by the time they arrived in Destin.

Not a small part of her tension was attributable to Max's family. She couldn't fault their hospitality. Obviously any friend of Max's was always welcome. And that was just it—she and Max were clearly more than friends, but the family treated her like a playmate the child Max might have brought home for the weekend.

She hoped she wouldn't have to see much of them, or Lydia.

THE NEXT FEW WEEKS were bliss. Samantha and Max were together every possible moment. He didn't refer to the weekend spent with his family, except to voice genuine thanks that it was over.

Given the rapid progress they had made in this romance, Samantha speculated that Stage Three would be upon them in no time, but as the days passed and the feelings they had for each other only seemed to grow deeper, she began to relax.

One night after a warm and wonderful round of lovemaking, curled up against his side, she told Max that she just couldn't understand why Stage Three was so long coming.

"Are you in such a hurry to find out all the bad things about me?" he asked.

"Of course not. It's just that...."

He interrupted her with a long lazy kiss. "Don't rush us through Stage Two, darlin', or we won't have time to enjoy it." His lips trailed across her cheek to her ear. He blew gently, sending the most delightful shivers down her spine. "Maybe we're one of those couples who is permanently hung up in this stage, darlin'," he murmured sleepily.

Samantha didn't say anything, but she knew that couldn't happen. She tried to hide her misgivings, but Max knew her too well, and he began to relieve her of small problems without her having to ask. When the kitchen sink backed up it was Max who called the plumber and made arrangements to meet him. When her checkbook refused to balance—something that had never happened before—Max picked her up out of her chair at the dining-room table, perched her on his lap and crooned in her ear while going over the figures until he found the check on which she had transposed the numbers. She decided that nurturing was very sexy.

He paid the utilities and the day-to-day running expenses of the condominium. She protested, but he pointed out reasonably that since they had no mortgage—she owned the property outright—it was only fair that he take on the responsibility for upkeep.

Samantha felt guilty. He was also paying for his room in the hotel. Finally she insisted that he move all his possessions into the condo and give up his room.

She ended up with most of the housekeeping duties, but she didn't mind. Her hours were not as long as Max's and he always pitched in to help when he was at home.

He was messy though, she was delighted to discover after only two days. The memory of that spotless hotel room had haunted her. Evidently he felt right at home here, because he certainly didn't bother to pick up after himself.

She was putting the fourth load of towels in the washing machine while he dressed. "How on earth do you manage to use so many towels?" she called through the bedroom door.

She was bending over, sorting the light colors from the dark and muttering to herself when he came up behind her. Suddenly she was lifted, turned, and found herself perched on top of the dryer.

"I'm very clean," Max informed her affably. His

hands were planted on each side of her. His jeans rode low on his hips and he hadn't put on his shirt. When she put out a hand to rake through the wiry hair on his bare chest he moaned softly. His hands slid under her bottom to urge her forward while his tongue probed the pulse at the base of her neck.

She laughed huskily and ran her hands with relish up the smooth skin of his shoulders, feeling the muscles flex as she scraped her nails lightly across them. "Clean, maybe, but not tidy," she told him.

He raised his head, a suggestion of laughter in his eyes. "Then I have a theory we should try out." His hands went to the buttons on the front of her shirt. Very slowly he opened them, one by one. He left a moist kiss on each bit of flesh as it was uncovered, his knuckles deliberately brushing her nipples.

"Wh-what is your theory?" Her breath caught in her throat making it extremely difficult for her to get the words out.

"The 'equal mess' theory. You throw your clothes on the floor and I'll pick them up." His voice was distracted. He finished with the last button and pushed back the sides of the shirt. "I wish you wouldn't wear a bra."

"I don't throw my clothes on the floor," she whispered, then added, "I have to wear one."

"Well then, I'll make your mess for you!" He stripped her shirt off and threw it over his shoulder. The bra followed quickly. "Yes, I suppose you do. For a little person you are generously endowed... and I love it," he rasped as his mouth sought one firm rosy nipple. He used his tongue to drive her to distraction.

Samantha arched her back to give him easier access. Her fingers, buried in his hair, tried to direct his lips to where she wanted them to go, but he teased and tormented until she was forced to beg. "Max, please."

Finally he relented, opening his mouth completely over the hard bud to suckle gently. He gathered her legs around his waist and picked her up with one arm beneath her derriere.

The towels were forgotten as he stepped over them on the way to the bedroom. Samantha was deposited carefully on the rumpled sheet. He reached for the elastic waistband of her shorts. "I like these little bitty shorts, but I don't want you wearing them outside," he said roughly. "They barely cover your behind."

"Yes, sir," she answered meekly.

He stripped off his jeans and joined her on the bed, arms drawing her against him. The passion in them built quickly to an explosive point, but when he would have moved over her, she pushed him off gently and sat up on her knees. His head fell back on the pillow, his pleased grin slightly off-center as she let her hands and lips bring him to the level of anticipation that threatened his iron control.

A deep sound, almost like an animal in pain, erupted from his throat, and he lifted her by the hips to lower her onto the shaft of his masculinity.

She caught her lip between her teeth and her eyes widened in wonder at the new and exciting sensation of freedom to move as she wished. Her rhythm was intuitive, leaving his hands free to caress her breasts.

"Ah, God, darlin'. That's good." His breathless

words increased the delightful feeling of power and her movements became bolder.

She watched through the screen of her lashes as his breathing accelerated and his head pushed back against the pillow. The vein in his neck began to throb wildly. Suddenly his hips surged upward catching her unawares. "Sam!" he shouted, and his long body shuddered convulsively. He gasped, reaching up to pull her down against him. "Oh, my love. Dammit. My little love." He groaned. His hands bit into her hips before moving restlessly and hungrily over her back, into her hair.

When he could breathe normally again he cradled her face in both hands and lifted her face to look into her eyes.

What he saw caused him to chuckle softly. "Babe, I'm sorry. Don't look so forlorn. Just give me a while and I'll make it up to you, I promise."

"Max?" She felt disoriented, awash on a sea of bewilderment. Though she didn't ask what had happened, he must have felt compelled to explain.

A large hand shoved her hair behind her shoulder. She noticed that his fingers trembled slightly. "Darlin', you got overenthusiastic, and I lost control."

She felt the heat rise in her cheeks and turned her face into his palm. "I'm sorry," she murmured.

"Don't apologize." He laughed. "It was fantastic, the most erotic experience of my life."

Her lips, still nestled against his hand, curved in a sly smile. "You liked it, did you?" she asked.

He frowned. "Don't get any ideas, Sam, my love. It couldn't have been very satisfying for you."

"Oh, I don't know. Power itself is an aphrodisiac,

and I kind of enjoyed having you in my power." Her lids drifted down as she remembered the heady feeling. She wiggled slightly.

Suddenly she found herself flat on her back. "Don't get used to it," he growled. His hips pressed the lower half of her body into the mattress.

Her eyes flew open. The face above her was filled with purpose and she felt the unexpected arousal grow against her thigh. "Max!" she whispered.

"This time I'm in charge," he declared.

She willingly gave him the power.

THEY SUNBATHED on the beautiful beach with its sand the consistency of sugar. Max bought her a sun hat with beer cans on it and she bought him a shirt with Panama Jack written down one sleeve. It was lavender. He protested at the color.

"You're crazy if you think I'm going to wear a lavender shirt," he told her in mock indignation.

She pretended to be hurt, hiding her expression beneath the brim of her beer-can hat. "I thought you'd like it because I picked it out."

He must have taken her seriously. "Darlin'. Of course I like it. See. I'm putting in on. It's a great shirt."

She dissolved into laughter.

They also bathed under the moon. Lying on the beach with her head on his stomach while Max pointed out the stars, she decided that moonbathing was more fun than sunbathing, and a lot cooler.

He told her wonderful mythological tales of the origin of the constellations. Later they danced on the edge of the sea to the music of the waves.

They shared the grocery bill. And going to the supermarket had never been so much fun. In fact, everything they did together was fun. How then could Samantha have foreseen the pain and unhappiness that was to come?

IT BEGAN INNOCENTLY. Her birthday was approaching and in a playful way she made sure Max knew the date. "But no surprises," she warned him during an early-morning walk on the beach. "I hate surprises."

"Where would you like to go to celebrate?" he asked.

The date fell on a Wednesday, which meant that they both had to work. "I'll let you take me dancing at the Dinner Club downstairs."

"Thank you," he answered with a grin. "You just want to get me into a monkey suit again." They had reached the headland that guarded the entrance to Choctawhatchee Bay and paused to watch a gleaming boat, on its way out into the gulf for a day's fishing, cut through the azure water. A dozen or more sport fishermen waved to them and they waved back.

"You looked very handsome in it," she mused as they turned to retrace their steps. She smiled up at him. "That night will always be one of my happier memories."

Max stopped to fix her with his gaze. The blue eyes flashed. "Mine, too." he admitted in a rough voice. "That was the night I first realized how very much I love you."

Samantha had never said the words. Her feelings for Max grew deeper and more meaningful each day, but she had never told him that she loved him. Perhaps it was time. She moved closer within the curve of his arm and opened her mouth to speak, but at that moment an older couple sauntering hand in hand in the other direction murmured a friendly greeting and Max answered with a smile. They lingered for a moment exchanging comments about the weather, the fishing prospects and the best places to eat in Destin.

Maybe she would tell him when they were back in the condominium.

When they had washed the sand from their feet and let themselves in, the telephone was ringing. Abe had a small emergency at Sea Tangle. Could Max come early today? The chance was lost, for the morning anyway, and when he left Samantha decided it was for the best. That commitment would be better made after they reached Stage Four: Deep and Everlasting Love, if they ever did.

THE BOOTH was the same and so was the waiter.

In a flood of nostaglia, Samantha had chosen to wear the same golden ensemble. Max was breathtakingly handsome in a tuxedo exactly like the one he'd ruined, the sun streaks in his brownish hair darkened by the shower he'd taken in the hotel's spa. She felt as if she was walking on a cloud as they crossed the lobby together. Actually, her life was so completely and wholly satisfying she looked gently upon the people around them, feeling sorry for those who weren't her.

The meal was superb; the band, splendid; Max, romantic. This might possibly be the most perfect night of her life.

And then Max dropped his bombshell in the form of a birthday present. The box should have warned her, but "Nice things come in small packages," she told him as she tore into the beautifully wrapped gift.

"They certainly do," he agreed, giving her a soft kiss on the side of her neck. He nodded to the waiter who lifted his hand to the band leader. The soft romantic strains of "The Anniversary Waltz" reached her ears at the same moment she lifted the lid of the padded box.

Of course, it was a ring. And of course, it was exquisite, a yellow diamond, oval in shape and surrounded by white diamond baguettes. As she looked down at the ring she blinked rapidly, trying to clear her eyes. In only a second she would have to meet his gaze. What would she say? Her throat closed on the now-familiar claustrophobic sensation.

Unfortunately she said the first thing that popped into her mind. "Why did you have to ruin it?"

A hard hand grasped her chin, forcing her face toward his. "Ruin it?" he asked in a choked voice, the muscle in his jaw jumping wildly. "Ruin it?" He was unbelieving. "My God, Samantha, marriage is the next logical step for us. Do you mean to tell me that you haven't seen that yet?"

"No. It isn't. We are so happy like we are. It isn't." The tears spilled. She couldn't stop them. They fell half in pain, half in anger, and when he read her expression a kaleidoscope of emotion crossed his features: raw hurt, defeat and finally despair.

As she watched, the tension in his jaw spread to his neck. She could see the artery clearly as it throbbed beneath the skin. His shoulders under the smoothly tailored jacket were stiff and rigid, as though by sheer willpower he held some dangerous force in check. The eyes, those beautiful eyes, which could be as blue as the sky on a summer day, took on the opaqueness and chill of ice frozen from aerated water. She didn't want to do this to him or to herself, but how could she agree to marriage when the very thought stifled and terrified her?

Very carefully she closed the lid on the box and replaced it on the table. Her fingers curled into fists and she dropped her eyes from the accusation in his.

"Time doesn't stand still, Samantha," he said raggedly. "Neither do relationships. If you try to freeze love where it stands it ends up stagnant and dead. You seem to be able to cope with everything except the future."

"That's not true!" she whispered, looking up.

"Isn't it? The time has come for a permanent commitment between us. I've made no secret of my love for you. And I think you love me, but suppose you tell me how you *do* feel."

"I love you, Max." The words were spoken at last, and Samantha's fists uncurled with the relief of finally having said them. "I really do. It's just that I'm not ready to make a decision like this."

Her confession did nothing to melt the ice in his eyes. "Do you have some sort of timetable in mind?" he asked sarcastically. "Tell me, Samantha. Do you think you might be ready for marriage, a commitment, a family, in a month? A year? Do you want to put an age limit on it? Say on your fortieth birthday? Do you think you will have worked up your courage by then?" His voice was rising, and he made a visible effort to control it. "The day I came home to find you in tears over an old movie, I thought I had finally broken through that practical shell you surround yourself with to find the romantic underneath, the woman brave enough to take a chance on her feelings. But I was wrong. The shell may have cracked but you're not about to let it open. You are an emotional coward, Dr. Hyatt. How long am I supposed to wait? Until the magic we have has faded to something more controllable? I won't do that. I won't stand by and see it turn to dust."

His sarcastic speech provoked stunned shock, as well as pain, a deep piercing pain. He didn't know her at all! Not at all! She wasn't like that! She wasn't an emotional coward—the phrase made her wince. She might have some things in her personality that needed working through but she had to have *time* for that.

This wasn't Max, not the loving Max, the gentle and patient man she'd grown to know, the one she was beginning to love. This man was a stranger. It occurred to her fleetingly, only to be dismissed, that the relentless unfeeling expression he wore might be a defensive reaction. No. He needed no defense against her. She had admitted her love, made herself vulnerable for the first time in her life, but she needed more time. Her anger began to build to meet that in his eyes. If he was too selfish to grant her the days, the weeks, maybe even months, that she needed, well, so what? She refused to rush into marriage. He'd known how she felt about that right from the very beginning.

"You're demanding a decision?" She lifted her chin.

He sighed, an immensely tired sound. His fingers played with a spoon for a minute, then tossed it away. "Yes, I suppose I am." He met her stare with deliberation.

"Well, I won't be delivered an ultimatum like some meek little harem girl who's expected to be grateful for a scrap from the master's table!" She scooted around the banquette and stood, her purse in her hand. "I have my car. If you'll excuse me...."

An unwilling smile lifted one corner of his mouth slightly. "It's now or never, Samantha. I love you but I'm not going to sit around on my hands waiting for you to drop a crumb from your table, either."

She hadn't thought there was any more room for surprises, but that statement delivered another. Did he believe that was what she wanted? To have him at heel like a well-trained puppy? She stared at him, her fingers opening and closing the clasp of her purse. When he pointedly drew her attention to the tiny nervous gesture with his eyes, she stopped immediately.

"Sit down again, Samantha. You aren't in that big a hurry." The note of command held a hint of steel as well. "Tell me, what are the signs of the end of a love affair?"

She sat down on the edge of the padded seat. The end? Did he really mean it? "What?" she whispered. Her lips seemed stiff and numb.

He slouched down in the seat, one hand in his pocket and picked up his wineglass with the other. Arm extended, he tilted the ruby-red liquid, watching its movement for a long quiet minute. Then he lifted it to his lips. "You've studied these relationships to such a great degree, I thought you'd be able to rattle them off," he said when he'd lowered the glass. "Shall I refresh your memory? Bitter arguments become more frequent. Dates are broken. Boredom sets in. Conversation is almost nonexistent. Sexual relations are halted. And finally other people enter the picture." He raised his eyes to meet hers. "Did I miss any?"

Dumbly she shook her head.

"Well, I'm telling you right now that I won't sit around and wait for those things to happen to us."

She found her voice. "Those things can happen just as easily in marriage as out of it."

Max straightened, resting both elbows on the table, and built a tower with his fingers. Stroking them across the mustache, he caught and held her gaze. "I don't happen to think they will. This has been an idyllic period, but as you predict in your Stage Three, it's time for reality. Stage Three itself isn't dangerous, Samantha. The people going through it are the danger. If they aren't strong enough, committed enough and enough in love...." He shrugged.

Samantha felt as though she were sliding down slick sides of a dark deep pit. She couldn't seem to grab a handhold to stop her progress so she just kept slipping farther and farther. "So it's marriage or nothing?" she whispered shakily.

He only hesitated for the blink of an eye before he nodded. His hand went to the back of his neck, massaging the muscles there.

In anyone else she would have interpreted the gesture as an anxious effort to relieve tension. But not from Max. He had begun this himself. "I don't want marriage."

The words came out as a plea for understanding and he searched her eyes for more information. "I'm just not ready, Max," she said again.

That strange tension in his shoulders held him motionless. "Am I going to be evicted?"

Move him out? Not have Max in her home, in her life? For a moment her eyes were stricken, clinging to his. She felt the blood drain from her face. But there was no encouragement in his gaze, no sympathy for her feelings at all. He was leaving this strictly up to her. She couldn't!

He didn't wait for her answer, seeming to realize that she had none. He simply repeated his words of a moment ago. "Yes, I suppose I am."

Samantha turned away, the need to escape uppermost in her mind, and her heart like lead in her chest. She had to get out of here. She had to get away by herself to think.

Her feet moved automatically, thank God. They took her in a winding path through the tables, across the carpeted floor to the door. And then their self-motion abandoned her. She froze in utter dismay, unable to move another inch.

Getting off the elevator, looking as sleek and elegant as a fashion model, was Lydia Stone. She was dressed in black, setting a striking contrast to her carelessly coiffed blond hair. "Hello, Samantha. How nice to see you again."

From some reserve deep within came a calm she'd not known she still possessed. "How are you, Lydia? I didn't know you were here."

"Oh, yes. I arrived yesterday. Didn't Max tell you? I saw him at lunch today."

"He must have forgotten," Samantha said weakly.

"I needed a rest and the two of you had talked so much about Sea Tangle I decided to see if it was as nice as you'd described it."

May my tongue be silenced forever, thought Samantha. But she had no such luck. "Max is inside. I'm having an early night, so if you'll excuse me?"

"Certainly. I'll probably see you tomorrow. Night." She turned to speak to the maître d'.

"Good night," choked Samantha. As she walked away she heard Lydia ask if she could be seated at Mr. Stanwood's table.

GOD! I'VE REALLY BLOWN IT NOW, *thought Max as he watched her walk away. Her proud carriage was as rigid and stiff as his own. Should I go after her,* he wondered. *No. She must make this decision on her own. But what if she couldn't do it alone? I'll have to begin from scratch and it won't be easy this time. It could very well prove to be impossible. She won't trust me an inch. Damn! Why did I crowd her?*

Because she wouldn't budge without it. Because he was an impatient fool. Because he had some kind of crazy idea that all she needed was a little push. He was so sure that she was ready, so *sure*. Because he wanted his wedding ring on her finger, wanted it with a desperation that he didn't understand.

When she was out of sight he picked up his wine goblet and drained it. His chin fell to his chest as he looked down into the glass feeling equally empty, equally drained. Moisture gathered behind his eyes. He thought about leaving. He didn't want to sit here in a public restaurant and cry. But he couldn't seem to move. To hell with it. At that moment he didn't give a damn what people in the Dinner Club thought of him. Only one person mattered and he'd chased her away.

He blinked and remembered Sam blinking the

same way before her tears fell. He ought to be shot or have his tongue cut out for making her cry. Beautiful, sexy, warm, loving Sam. At the image of her gorgeous body curved in sleep next to him he almost groaned aloud. He should be thinking about where he was going to sleep tonight but he didn't give a damn about that, either. He'd made some colossal mistakes in his life but this one topped them all.

The waiter appeared. "Can I refill your glass, sir?"

Without speaking Max extended it. "When the band comes back have them play that song again," he murmured in a desultory tone.

"'The Anniversary Waltz,' sir?"

He picked up the box that Samantha had left on the table. Flipping back the lid he stared at the ring, remembering how he had thought of her eyes when he'd seen it. "Yeah. Have them play it again." He took a long swallow from the refilled glass and slipped the box into his pocket. He crumpled the foil wrapping paper in his fist.

"Max?"

At the sound of the feminine voice his head jerked upright, his eyes bright with hope.

It was only Lydia, he realized, and slumped again.

Lydia? He sat up. "What are you doing here?" he asked suspiciously.

She subsided gracefully on the padded cushion and nodded to the waiter. "I'm here for a vacation." Taking the menu from his hand, she scanned it quickly and ordered. "If you have another glass, I'll have some of that lovely Beaujolais." She smiled at the man and he hastened to do her bidding. "I saw you today at lunch, but you were very busy," she told Max over the rim of her glass.

"Yes," he answered shortly. "Did the family send you here?"

"Naturally," she told him easily. "They think I still have some influence on you."

His eyes narrowed, taking in the clinging dress, the hair, the makeup. Lydia was always well-groomed but tonight she had gone further, making herself deliberately seductive. The lawyer in him whispered caution. "Do they?" he asked blandly.

She shrugged her beautiful shoulders and managed to cloud her eyes with sadness. "Of course, they don't know that I never did have any influence."

"No, Lydia. You're not going to lay that guilt at my feet. You didn't love me any more than I loved you. It was a business proposition."

She avoided his eyes. "Maybe it was...at first," she said softly. "Are you going to marry her?"

Max schooled his features to soften the pain of hearing his answer voiced. "I asked her. She said no."

Lydia looked up. "Then, maybe—"

"God!" he interrupted harshly. "Do you have no feelings?"

"I'm not thinking of us, Max. I'm thinking of the firm. We really need you back."

"Any lawyer on the East Coast would be grateful to work for the firm. You can have your pick of the best."

"Ah, yes," she acknowledged. "But the best whose name happens to be Stanwood is another matter. Max, how can you turn your back on what your grandfather worked so hard to build?"

"You know how. There are enough high profiles in my family."

"But to give it all up to become a bartender?" She clearly thought he was insane.

Maybe he was. "As a matter of fact, I'm thinking of returning to practice."

Lydia leaned forward in her excitement. "Max... !"

He held up a hand. "Here in Destin. A one-man office on a small scale."

Shaking her head in disgust, she relaxed against the cushion. "What a waste of a fine mind."

"I don't happen to think so," he said coolly. "That's where we finally differed, Lydia. I discovered that I'd rather practice for the love of the law. You'd find it boring if you couldn't mix in politics and power plays."

She looked up to meet his eyes. "What about Samantha?"

The muscle in his jaw jumped involuntarily. "What about her?" he grated.

"You said she'd refused your proposal. Destin's a small town. Won't you be uncomfortable running into her on the street?" She reached over to cover his hand where it rested on the table between them.

He looked down at the long fingers, the red pointed nails and felt a sudden wave of nausea sweep over him. He recognized the aversion to another woman's touch and moved his hand.

But the withdrawal didn't deter Lydia. "Think about it, Max. You're a brilliant attorney. She plays piano in a bar."

Max looked at her in stunned surprise.

She went on without pausing. "A luxury-resort bar but still a bar. She's a lightweight, Max. You'd be bored stiff in a year."

Shock reddened her face when he threw back his

head and began to laugh. He listened to the sound himself wondering if the disorder of his emotions was coming through in the laughter.

A MIRACLE BROUGHT SAMANTHA to her door. Later she was unable to remember anything about the drive from Sea Tangle to Holiday Isle. She lay on her bed, still dressed in the golden silk, and tried to recall putting the key in the ignition, turning the steering wheel, but it was all a blank.

And she couldn't cry. That was the worst part. Tears would have been a release, but this hurt went far too deep for tears. Numbed and bewildered by the emotions of the past few hours, she turned onto her side, automatically putting out a hand for the large male body that should be there.

Where was he?

How could he do this to her?

Where was he?

SAMANTHA SPENT A SLEEPLESS NIGHT, and when dawn arrived it was with a feeling akin to relief that she dragged herself out of bed. Three cups of coffee failed to disperse her lethargy.

She should get dressed. She should be making some kind of plans, she told herself wearily. But then she asked herself why? Why did it seem imperative that she make plans, and what for? Plans were for future events and as far as she could see there was no future for her.

She poured her fourth cup of coffee and took it out onto the balcony. A warm breeze off the ocean molded the silk of her gown and negligee to her curves. The brush of the fabric against her skin sensitized her nipples, her thighs. She hugged her arms underneath her breasts to ward off the sudden flood of desire.

Max had given her an ultimatum; she had rejected it, and Lydia had been waiting to step in.

How was she going to get through today? She would have loved to call Sea Tangle to tell Anna that she was sick. But today was Thursday, her regular day to play piano for little Janie. Only the memory of the child's eyes, watching so carefully as Samantha's fingers moved over the keys of the piano, stopped her. With a tired sigh she sank back against the yellow cushions of a chaise longue.

Janie had still not spoken nor touched the keys herself, but her constantly darting eyes were at rest while she watched and listened. Samantha couldn't take that progress lightly, aware of how much patience it had taken to get even this far with Janie.

How could she stand to be in the same room with Max for four and a half hours? Knowing how her music always reflected her emotions, how could she play songs that wouldn't reveal how desolate she was? If only she could get really angry at him, maybe this aching would go away.

She paused with the cup halfway to her lips and tried. He knew. He knew exactly how she felt, but he thought it was her fault, that she was a coward, so he showed no mercy.

Lydia's arrival was perfectly timed—she added that other item to her sour thoughts. Max hadn't even mentioned it to her. Why? Either he didn't think it was important or he was holding Lydia in reserve while he delivered his demands to Samantha. In her research she had come upon timing as a factor in romantic relationships. Often a man or woman would come to a point in his or her life when subconsciously he or she was ready for commitment.

If Max had reached such a time in his life he might be devastated for a while because he thought Samantha was the only one for him. But eventually he would discover that another woman would do just as well.

She added betrayal to his sins. Damn him! If he was that untrustworthy she didn't need him anyway!

Setting the cup down on a convenient table at her elbow, she stood and began to pace restlessly. Anger wasn't working.

She realized that her thoughts were irrational and fluctuating and totally unreasonable, but she couldn't seem to get them onto a path where anything made sense. She hurt so. She ran her fingers into her hair and pulled hard. The pain brought tears to her eyes but it didn't open the floodgates as she hoped it would. She needed to cry. Needed it desperately. But the tears remained locked somewhere deep within her heart.

The doorbell interrupted her pacing. She looked at the wooden barrier accusingly. Then her heart speeded up to an alarming rate. It was Max, had to be. He had no clothes except his tux, and he couldn't go to work in black tie. For the hundredth time she wondered where he had spent the night.

She approached the door slowly, palms clammy and throat dry. Just before she reached for the knob she looked down at what she was wearing and groaned. Why hadn't she dressed? He would think she had deliberately kept on the slinky outfit. Then she had another horrible thought. Max had a key. He wouldn't ring the bell. What if he'd sent Lydia to pick up his clothes? He wouldn't be so cruel... would he? Why hadn't the stupid manager of this stupid condominium installed a peep hole?

She jerked open the door, and then had to hold onto the knob to stay upright. It was Max and he looked as bad as she felt. As her gaze took in the rumpled black pants and wrinkled shirt she couldn't help remembering one other day when the tuxedo was the only thing he had to wear. A picture of a happier Max, running flat out down the beach, pant legs rolled up, merged with a memory of walking arm in arm in the rain, stopping to kiss, laughing....

"May I come in?"

"Oh." She jumped, startled out of her reverie. "Yes, of course."

He paused on the threshold. "Are you all right, Samantha?" he asked quietly.

She looked up at him blindly. "I—I'm fine," she whispered.

With a helpless groan he closed the door behind him and pulled her into his arms, his chin resting on her head.

The tender embrace was her undoing. Finally the tears fell; he held her, stroking her hair, while her heart emptied itself. He didn't tell her not to cry, thank goodness.

There are a limited number of tears in a person, surely, but Samantha had no idea how long she cried. When she reached the hiccupping stage Max maneuvered her into the guest bath and grabbed for a handful of tissue.

She mopped her eyes and blew her nose, then tried to laugh. "A hero is always supposed to have a handkerchief."

"But I'm not a hero, darlin'. I'm just a man who has made you very unhappy, and I'm sorry for it."

Wet eyes lifted to his. "Oh, no, Max. You didn't make me unhappy. I did that to myself."

His smile was infinitely sad as he tucked a thick swath of auburn hair behind her ear. His eyes roamed her face as though to memorize her features. She wanted to smooth away the deep lines on either side of his mouth, but she was afraid to touch him.

"Our timing was off," he said softly.

The book again. She could no longer resist. Raising her fingers to his face she murmured, "No, Max. It's me. My timing will probably never be on for marriage. You were right. I'm a coward."

The expressions that chased across his face served to deepen the lines even further. His pain was evident in the tightening of his lips, the twisting of his brows, and in his eyes...she could hardly bear to look into his eyes.

He seemed to grab for control. A deep breath, a visible straightening of his shoulders, and he had a tenuous hold. "Samantha, I'm going back to Jacksonville. For a little while anyway. Then I'll probably look for another small town to open a practice. I want you to know where I am if you ever need me, so I'll keep Abe and Anna informed."

She nodded, unable to speak.

"I'll have the movers call you about getting my stuff out and bringing your bed back."

"Where did you spend the night?" She heard the words but had no idea where they came from.

He met her horrified expression with a weak smile and a shake of his head. "On the beach," he said at last.

"Oh."

"Lydia—"

"She came to get you back," she said quickly. She really felt that she should warn him.

"I know. The firm will collapse if another Stanwood isn't there to prop it up," he said sarcastically.

She started to tell him that it wasn't the firm who wanted him, but stopped herself just in time to keep from sounding like a jealous shrew. It wasn't her business. Besides, she wanted Max to be happy, didn't she? If Lydia was the one who could make him happy then she should have him. Her fingers curled into fists.

That was a big "if," though. Lydia would make him work too hard, she would get him involved in politics again, and he didn't need that. She put a brake on her thoughts. Who was she to decide what Max needed? "Why didn't you tell me yesterday that she was here?"

"I didn't know until last night. You had already left."

Samantha gave a snort of disbelief. "I saw her as I was leaving. She said you knew." Was that her voice sounding so petulant, so agitated?

"She wants you back for herself." Now she *really* hadn't meant to say *that*. She whirled away so he wouldn't see her embarrassment.

"I'll always love you, Samantha." The words were spoken in a whisper, but they were strong nonetheless.

"Then, why...? I'll always love you, Max," she cried, wringing her hands together in an age-old gesture of desperation. "Why are we doing this to each other? We were so happy. Can't we just go on living together?"

He shook his head. "It wouldn't work for me, darlin'." His voice held a note of depressing finality. "Every time I'd look at you I'd want to see my ring on your finger, my child at your breast. I'd eventually begin to resent you for not giving me those things."

She let her head fall forward, the cloud of hair hiding her face.

Max cleared his throat, and his voice was a husky murmur when he spoke again. "I need to pack a bag and get going. I'm working the lunch shift. Abe has someone coming in tonight to take over my job."

So this was the last time she'd see him, she thought, watching the broad shoulders disappear through the door to their bedroom—no, her bedroom.

It didn't take him long to pack the shaving things in the bathroom, his clothes from the bureau, then move to the guest-room closet. He swept the hangers into a fist and slung them over his shoulder. His other hand held the suitcase.

She had stood in the tiny hallway, watching helplessly as he progressed from room to room. Now he returned to stand before her. "Goodbye, Samantha, my love," he murmured and bent to brush her lips with his one last time. "If you change your mind...." Their eyes met, their lips curved in dismal melancholy smiles.

She was going to miss the mustache, she thought irrelevantly. "Bye, Max," she whispered faintly.

"Can you get the door for me?" he asked.

"What? Oh, sure." She opened it wide and he was gone.

THE PIANO BAR off the lobby at Sea Tangle was empty except for Janie and her grandmother. Samantha made a conscious effort to keep her eyes away from the bar. She could not imagine what it would do to her later to see another man there.

When Max had left this morning she had felt the bottom drop out of her world with the closing of the door. All day she had paced the length and breadth of the apartment, knowing herself for the coward he had called her, but unable to do anything about the condition.

"What a lovely dress, Samantha." Anna smiled.

"Thank you," Samantha said softly. The dress was one she hadn't worn before. A cocktail-length hyacinth chiffon over a fragile slip of dark purple, it was cut on simple lines with straight long sleeves and a high neckline, and fastened at the neck and waist with tiny hooks. There were no closures in between so a strip of bare skin teased the eye from the back. Her newly acquired tan glowed through the sheer fabric.

"I've always thought that shade looks so pretty on women with your coloring." Anna's voice faded off on the last word. "Is there anything wrong, dear?"

Samantha's lips parted and closed again. She swallowed hard and looked at Anna, unable to hide her unhappiness.

"It's Max, isn't it?" the older woman asked.

Samantha nodded, her eyes shimmering with misery.

"Oh, my dear, I should have warned you. Max is a love. He has been wonderful for Abe and me. But, Samantha, he will never be marriage material." She shook her head sadly. "He's just not the type for home and hearth." She put her hand on Samantha's arm. "I feel so guilty for not having said something sooner."

Samantha knew that her face registered blank surprise.

"You are too upset today to play for Janie. Would you like to take the night off? I'll fix it with Abe."

Still unable to get words past the lump in her

throat, Samantha shook her head vigorously, but Anna ignored her. She kept up a rambling chatter as she took Janie's hand and started to lead her away. "If you are worried about your job, don't be. I'll explain everything to my husband. He'll understand."

"No." At first Samantha thought the word had come from her own mouth. It sounded so lost, so pitiful.

"Please." It was a weak whisper from the frail child between them, and for a long second the two women stared at each other. Then their eyes moved as one to the white pinched face that looked up at Samantha with such longing.

Her own troubles forgotten, Samantha sank to her knees and held out her arms. Janie came into them with no hesitation whatever. Anna joined them, tears streaming down her cheeks. Her hand went out to rest in a tender caress on her granddaughter's back.

"No, no, sweetheart. I'm not going anywhere." Samantha managed to find her voice as she laid her cheek on Janie's head. "We'll have our songfest just as we always do. We'll play 'Pop, Goes the Weasel.' And today your grandmother will stay to hear us. Is that okay?" These tears were tears of joy, and Samantha released them gratefully. They wet the little head in a baptism of loving relief.

Janie pulled out of Samantha's arms and turned to reach for her grandmother. "Stay," she murmured in her rusty croak.

Anna's arms convulsed around the child. "Thank God," she whispered. "Oh, sweetheart, I'd love to stay."

An hour later Samantha looked up impatiently as

a customer entered the lounge. Anna caught her eye and smiled. "We have to go now, sweetheart, so Samantha can play for all the other people who want to hear her."

Janie slipped off the piano bench where she had sat close beside Samantha, and gave a quiet smile.

The loss of the heat from the tiny body went through Samantha, leaving a sudden chill. "I'll see you on Monday," she said to the child.

Janie reached out one finger and touched a white key of the piano, very softly, very carefully. The note was almost lost in the breathless silence of the room, but its echo lingered in the air long after Janie had taken her grandmother's hand to be led away.

Samantha sat looking down at the key. She would never have any children. Never have a warm little body cuddle close in search of love or need. Never experience the joy of sharing parenthood with the man she loved. Never even waken next to him in the night seeking love and comfort for herself. Her life stretched in front of her, lonely and barren. Because she was a coward. She couldn't blame her parents for her fear of divorce forever. The cowardice was in herself. Life didn't hand out any guarantees. Only Max's love could banish her particular fears. And it would, she realized, with a sudden rush of feeling. His love was strong enough to lighten any burden that weighted her; hers was powerful enough to comfort him, too, when the world closed in. Without him she was half a person. That was the lesson he'd tried to teach her, and she'd been too stubborn to accept it.

Her eyes went to the mahogany bar. A stranger was there, talking to Barbara and Jenny, an interloper. She looked blindly around the room. Several more customers had gathered and were watching her expectantly, but she only noted their presence with a vacant stare. Her mind was working furiously.

She was a fool. A first-class fool who had been about to drown in her own stupidity and stubbornness. She didn't know the meaning of the word *love*. Love was giving, and she had done nothing but take from Max, unwilling even to give him commitment, the only thing he'd ever asked of her.

She had sat in the ivory tower of isolation and theorized about the stages of romance as though she had all the answers, as though she alone knew what real love was. And she was wrong, criminally, bitterly wrong.

Mentally she threw her precious book in the ash can and squared her shoulders. If she left right after work she could be in Jacksonville before dawn. Max would forgive her. He *had* to. She pulled the microphone toward her lips. "Good evening, ladies and gentlemen. My name is Samantha Hyatt...."

IT WAS AFTER EIGHT when Max stood on the step at the entrance to the lounge. He paused, looking around. *Samantha must be taking a break,* he thought in relief. Abe and Anna had invited him for a farewell drink, but he dreaded the experience. Being in the same room with Samantha? How could he stand it? Then again, how could he refuse those two when they had done so much for him? His gaze found their favorite table to be empty and he glanced at his watch. He was early.

"Max, come sit with me."

He knew the source of the request before he turned. Lydia. He considered ignoring her. She had made such a pest of herself about his going back to Jacksonville that he'd agreed to return for a visit until he could decide where to settle. Lydia was right about one thing: he could not remain in Destin, not as long as Samantha was here. Finally he shrugged and walked over. "Hello, Lydia," he said indifferently.

SAMANTHA ENTERED to settle herself at the piano. She hadn't even touched the keys when she heard the ripple of Lydia's laughter mingled with the deeper tones of Max's. He hadn't gone!

The leap that her heart took fell very short, however. Lydia had a possessive grip on his arm that would have rivaled a hold on "Saturday Night Wrestling."

Samantha frowned at the woman, but her jealous glare was totally wasted. The lovely lawyer's complete attention was focused on her handsome male companion. Desperate measures, such as smooth harmonies and provocative lyrics, were called for under these circumstances.

She raced through her mental repertoire and came up with several, which she wove into a medley. "Night and Day" melted into "What is This Thing Called Love?"

Max glanced over his shoulder, his expression unreadable.

"Body and Soul" gave way to "Lover, Come Back to Me." How could those songs possibly fail to touch his heart, to evoke the pictures she intended? "September in the Rain" became "Stormy Weather" to remind him of the rainy day on the beach. If he was stirred in any way by the music he couldn't help but remember, too, the hours afterward when they had made love to the rhythms of rain drumming on the balcony.

She played and sang, on and on, drawing forth all the ballads of forever love she could think of. Max's back remained firmly turned toward the piano, but were his shoulders just a little bit stiff?

Abe and Anna came in and joined the pair at the small round table. Conversation was lively for a minute. Samantha wondered if Anna was telling the other couple about the breakthrough with Janie this afternoon.

Lydia said something that provoked a worried glance from Abe, and Anna tried not to look pitying while they both turned their attention to Samantha. All she earned from Max was an occasional glimpse of his piercing blue eyes.

The minutes dragged by. Samantha looked at her watch: eight forty-five. If she hadn't had a reaction from him by now, she feared there wouldn't be one.

When Lydia and Max stood up to leave, Samantha was devastated. She had lost, failed. In her insolent assurance she'd thought all she had to do was crook a finger and he would come running. She should have known better. Max Stanwood was his own man, not one to cater to the whims of a vacillating woman who couldn't make up her mind.

She watched him put a lacy shawl across the bare shoulders and, with a hand in the small of her back, escort Lydia away in the direction of the elevators.

She never knew what possessed her to do it. It was not a conscious decision, but as she bent to peek through the fronds of a fern, she could see them talking earnestly as they waited for the car to descend to the lobby. Her fingers struck the keys one more time in the poignant and sorrowful old American folk tune, later rewritten by W. C. Handy, that tells the story of the unfortunate fertility of an unmarried southern mountain girl.

Max whirled and his gaze blazed through the plants, scorching her where she sat. He couldn't possibly see her, she told herself apprehensively, shrinking from the force of his glare. Could he? Had she gone too far?

The elevator doors opened and Max and Lydia stepped inside as the last words of "Careless Love" faded away.

All the things inside Samantha that kept her going—her heart, her lungs, her brain—shut down at one time, leaving only a numb shell of a woman. It took her several minutes to calm her shaking hands so that she could go into her final theme song.

Tonight the words had never seemed so appropriate. "Smoke Gets in Your Eyes" was as good an excuse for the tears as any. And she really needed an excuse, for her friends—Jenny standing beside the bar twisting a towel in her hands; Abe and Anna, trying to keep the polite smiles on their faces—were commiserating silently. Even Barbara, who had never shown any affection for Samantha at all, was subdued as she watched.

If they kept this up she would never get out of here without disgracing herself. She didn't want to do anything as inappropriate and unbecoming as to cry in public, but there didn't seem to be a way out of it.

Suddenly there was a commotion at the door. Two men who happened to be leaving were split apart by a very determined and very angry Max.

He stalked across the room, headed directly toward the piano. There was murder in his eye.

He was furious! "Careless Love" probably hadn't been such a good idea, thought Samantha anxiously. She blinked the tears away—one rolled down each cheek—and played a repeat chorus of her theme song. Maybe the extra minutes would give him time to calm down.

Max loomed over the keyboard, waiting for her to finish. She shot a quick glance upward to see the muscle in his jaw throb beneath the skin. Instead of being calmed by the forced wait, he seemed to grow more and more impatient, more and more angry. Finally she struck the last notes and sighed heavily. Her eyes were wide with apprehension when she met the ice-blue stare.

"Samantha, are you pregnant?" he asked bluntly, holding her gaze and making no effort to lower his voice.

Her jaw dropped but she recovered to answer instantly, "No."

All the stiffness seemed to go out of his knees. He sat on the bench next to her and stared at her as though she'd lost her mind. "Then why...?"

Belatedly Samantha looked around to see that the customers in close proximity to the table were grinning with very knowing expressions.

"Max, please..." she started to say, only to feel a hard hand around her wrist. She was pulled to her feet without ceremony.

"Let's get out of here," he growled.

She grabbed for her purse as he started through the crowd with her in tow. There was nothing gentle about the way he was hauling her out of the lounge, but she wouldn't have cared if he had hauled her through the gates of hell.

They passed a worried-looking Abe and Anna on their way out of the lounge. Samantha managed a reassuring smile. She wasn't really sure whether she should be reassured or not, but he was here, not with Lydia, and he was touching her.

She had to run to keep up with him or else have her arm wrenched from its socket. The very proper doorman saw them coming and raised a disapproving brow. Then the poor man realized that if he didn't get those doors open Max was liable to go through them closed. He swung them both wide, just in case.

Max dragged her through the double doors, muttering under his breath, and across the asphalt drive until they reached his car.

He pulled her even with him and propped her against the fender. "Now, Samantha. Would you like to explain your behavior?"

"Why did you leave with Lydia?" she parried.

"She asked me to see her to her room," he answered abstractedly.

His mind was clearly not on Lydia, and Samantha gave a wry smile.

"'Lover, Come Back to Me.' My God! What the hell were you trying to do to me?" He jerked his tie free of its knot—she wondered who had tied it—and opened the top button of his shirt. "Are you still playing games?"

She opened her mouth to explain.

But he didn't wait for an explanation. "Listen to me," he demanded, planting his fists on his lean hips. He had never looked so wonderful. Even with the scowl across his brow he was sexy and handsome and masculine, and she loved every inch of the huge body.

She closed her mouth again, willing to hear whatever he had to say. But she did put a hand on his broad chest. The gesture had all the effect she could have wished for. A great shudder ripped through him like a concussion.

"Dammit!" he roared and took a step away. Her hand fell to her side. "Samantha Hyatt, you are the most maddening woman. What the hell was the melodrama we played out this morning? A new and subtle form of torture you dreamed up? I can't take any more of it. Are you going to marry me or not?" He was shouting now, and the doorman had moved out from his post in order to see better.

Samantha decided that it was her turn to take this step, toward him. "Oh my darling, I thought you'd never ask...again," she murmured, her whiskey voice thick with relief and excitement.

He stared at her dumbfounded and backed up.

She followed relentlessly and wound her arms around his neck to tug his head down. "I love you. I've loved you from the first moment your eyes zapped me."

Such a short distance between their lips, but it might as well have been the width of an ocean. He wasn't giving an inch. "You haven't answered me," he said. The demand was meant to be delivered in the same harsh tone, but Samantha noticed that his voice was ragged and husky.

Her lips curved in a delicious smile and she stood on tiptoe to brush them over the cleft in his chin. "Yes, I'll marry you. Tonight if you can find a preacher. But we're throwing away the book."

Suddenly his arms convulsed to sweep her feet from the ground. Her mouth was captured in a kiss of the deepest hunger she'd ever known. He wound one hand in her hair to force her head closer and devoured her lips as though he would never have enough of the taste of her. When he released her to take a breath he buried his face against the curve of her neck with what sounded strangely like a sob. "Don't you ever leave me, Samantha Hyatt." It was both a demand and a plea.

"And don't you ever leave me, Max Stanwood." Her fingers wove through the cool strands of his hair. "Even when I'm completely unreasonable, please don't give up on me, my love."

THREE DAYS LATER, on Sunday, Max stood in front of the wide glass window in the lounge at Sea Tangle and looked around at the friends gathered there. Furniture had been removed to provide an aisle. Flowers were banked to frame, but not hide, the sun-splashed view of the ocean.

A cassock-clad minister stood at Max's shoulder, and Abe was by his side. His family was here, too, his brother very put out at not being asked to be the best man.

They had drafted the keyboard man from the Rural Route to take Samantha's accustomed place at the piano, and he was playing softly in the background while they waited.

Minutes passed and Max began to fidget. Where

was she? The assembled guests were whispering to each other and looking over their shoulders.

Not having any family of her own, Samantha had chosen to give herself away, to walk to him alone. Now he panicked. His hands inside the gray gloves began to perspire. The high collar of the morning suit chafed at his neck. He should have *made* her have someone. What if she got cold feet at the last minute?

A terrible fear gripped him and he muttered to Abe, "Hold the fort. I'll be right back." He strode to the entrance.

She was just getting out of the elevator, one hand gripping the nosegay he'd chosen, the other holding up the skirts of the beautiful wedding gown of softest ivory. A short veil hid her eyes from him and the small barrier annoyed him unreasonably. He crossed the lobby in long steps. "Dammit, Samantha. Where the hell have you been? Every one of those people in there thinks you've stood me up."

She thrust the bouquet at him. "Oh, Max. Thank goodness you're here. I couldn't find anything blue. You'd think Anna would have *something* blue, wouldn't you? I didn't want to go rummaging through her drawers. But you're going to have to get me something." All the while she spoke she was arranging the hem of her dress to her satisfaction. She gave it a final twitch and straightened to take the flowers from his hand.

"Something blue? You want something blue? Now?" A half smile tilted the mustache as he looked down at his tiny beloved.

She nodded. "Please," she said as though it was the most reasonable request in the world.

He knew the rhyme, of course, and if his Samantha wanted something blue to complete her bridal outfit, she would have it. With two fingers he lifted a corner of the veil to look into her eyes. Their expression made him catch his breath and warmed him so thoroughly that he knew he'd never be cold again.

"You got it," he told her tenderly and stole a quick kiss.

"Max," she chided gently. "You're not supposed to do that."

"Be right back." He turned and walked back to the lounge. Standing in the entrance, he let his eyes scan the room until he found the person he was looking for. He threaded his way through the baffled guests until he reached his brother. "Do you still wear those awful blue suspenders?" he asked.

His brother sputtered. "Well, yes. But, Max, what on earth...?"

"Give them to me," Max demanded.

"I can't do that!"

"You're sitting down. You won't lose your pants and I need them. Now." He had already pushed aside his brother's jacket and was reaching for the teethed fasteners in the back.

"Thanks," he said to the beet-red face a moment later and headed back into the lobby.

When Samantha saw what he had in his hand she almost dropped her flowers. "Max, what...how...?" she asked helplessly.

"Samantha, I'm in a great hurry to marry you and my family has finally contributed something of value to this occasion. Now turn around."

He burrowed up under the billowing skirts to tie

the elastic strips around her waist. He gave her rounded bottom a light pinch for good measure.

"Your father?" she asked, grinning over her shoulder at him.

"My brother," he corrected as he stood.

"Max." She put out a hand to stop him before he could return to the lounge. "Your family contributed the most valuable part of this occasion," she said softly.

He gripped her hand tightly but could not control the tremor in his voice. "I was wrong about you, Samantha. You're a dyed-in-the-wool romantic."

"Yes," she acknowledged with a delighted smile. "I think I am."

"Let's go in together," he said, placing her hand in the crook of his arm.

There was one final surprise for Samantha as they reached the altar. Scored in the sand beyond the window, in letters ten feet long, were the words, I LOVE YOU, SAM STANWOOD.